The Death
of Sigmund Freud

The Death
of Sigmund Freud

*Fascism, Psychoanalysis
and the Rise of Fundamentalism*

Mark Edmundson

BLOOMSBURY

First published in Great Britain 2007

Copyright © 2007 by Mark Edmundson

Bloomsbury Publishing Plc
36 Soho Square
London W1D 3QY

www.bloomsbury.com

Bloomsbury Publishing, London, New York and Berlin

A CIP catalogue record for this book is available from the British Library

ISBN 9780747586074

10 9 8 7 6 5 4 3 2 1

Typeset by Hewer Text UK Ltd, Edinburgh
Printed in Great Britain by Clays, St Ives plc

The paper this book is printed on is certified by the © 1996 Forest Stewardship Council A.C. (FSC). It is ancient-forest friendly. The printer holds FSC chain of custody SGS-COC-2061

FSC
Mixed Sources
Product group from well-managed
forests and other controlled sources
Cert no. SGS-COC-2061
www.fsc.org
© 1996 Forest Stewardship Council

For Willie, fellow maker

I
Vienna

In the late autumn of 1909, two men who would each transform the world were living in Vienna, Austria. They were in almost every way what the poet William Blake would have called "spiritual enemies." One was Sigmund Freud, the creator of psychoanalysis, who would become the most renowned and controversial thinker of the twentieth century. In 1909, Freud was in vigorous middle age, fifty-three years old and at the height of his powers. The other man, whose impact on humanity would be yet greater, was young.

The young man had come to Vienna in hopes of making his fortune as an architect and an artist. He lived with a friend in a small apartment, and there he spent his time reading, drawing, writing, composing music, and dreaming of future triumphs. The young man had inherited a small sum of money when his mother died, and on these funds he lived frugally, eating little and paying modest rent. His main indulgence was opera, Wagner's opera in particular. There were disappointments: he was rejected not once but twice by the state-sponsored art school, and this infuriated him. He had never gotten along well with teachers, and the faculty at the art school was no exception—they sneered at his work and told him that he had no real talent. The young man decided to take up a bohemian life and to succeed brilliantly as an architect, and perhaps as a painter, poet, and composer too, despite Austria's corrupt establishment.

Before he left for Vienna, the young man fell in love with a woman named Stefanie, whom he saw on the evening walks he took back in his home city of Linz. Though he never spoke a word to Stefanie, the young man was faithful. All the glories he would achieve in the city, he hoped to lay before her in tribute. So even in decadent Vienna, he tried to lead a moral life: he stayed away from prostitutes; he stayed away from women in general, despite the fact that they often found him alluring. They stared at him at the opera and sent him notes requesting liaisons. But the young man was determined to keep what he called his "Flame of Life" pure.

From his boyhood, the young man was hypersensitive, prone to tantrums and bouts of weeping. He loved animals and could not bear to hear about any cruelty being inflicted on them, much less to see such a thing. He never drank and was sure that tobacco destroyed a person's health. He thought of himself as a humanitarian with a poetic nature. One of his major projects in Vienna was to design spacious, light-filled housing for the workers who lived in the city's slums, but no one outside his household ever saw the plans.

Soon the one friend that the young man had in Vienna went back home to the provinces, and by the time his friend returned, the young man had left their shabby apartment, giving the landlady no forwarding address. He became lost, lonely, and his money all but ran out. For a while he lived on the street, sleeping in doorways and on park benches. Perhaps at times he was compelled to beg. Finally, he found a home in a men's shelter, a strictly run, almost monastic establishment. Here he lived until a year before the beginning of the First World War, taking a certain kind of pleasure in the simplicity and order that now surrounded him. He made his living by painting postcards, which sold at kiosks on the street. He read a great deal, though he did not always understand what he read, and he gave speeches to the other residents of the shelter. He stood in the dayroom and held forth about the Jews and the Communists and about Germany's exalted destiny among nations. Sometimes one of his fellow residents would secretly tie his coat to the bench he was sitting on, and then provoke him with a political question. The young man would leap up then, and begin pacing around the room, declaiming, while the bench clunked along behind him. People who met the man sometimes had doubts about his sanity: none of them imagined that Adolf Hitler, for that, of course, is who the young man was, would ever be of consequence in the world.

Sigmund Freud was in the prime phase of his life when Hitler was living in Vienna. In middle age, Freud was a robust, full-faced man with a burgher's well-insulated body and a dense, regal brown beard, streaked with gray. His usual facial expression somehow conveyed both contentment and ambition. He had a hawk nose and bright, all-consuming eyes. Freud was not tall, only about five feet, seven inches, but his presence was formidable: he seemed to be more than a match for life. In his fifties, Freud looked like a field marshal of intellect—worldly, urbanely humorous, and self-aware.

In the fall of 1909, when Hitler was living on the streets, Freud was emerging from a protracted period of isolation. He had undergone an intense self-analysis; he had composed and published his first major work, *The Interpretation of Dreams*; and he was well begun in his exploration of the unconscious. Now Freud was writing constantly: he believed that once one understood the nature of the id—or the "it"—and its conflicted relation to the conscious mind, many previously puzzling matters in human life became understandable. Freud could offer unexpected truths not only about dreams, but also about jokes and slips of the tongue and pen. He had illuminating ideas about art, religion, the sources of human identity, and a great deal more. Now, after Freud had struggled for many years to distinguish himself, brilliant younger men, and some gifted women as well, were gathering around him. He was creating something like a movement.

As a young man, Freud confessed that he wanted to take on the major questions. He secretly aspired to be something of a philosophe, in the manner of Diderot, Rousseau, and Voltaire, and to make original contributions on matters like free will and fate, just government, love and death, and the good life. Finally, Freud believed that he had put himself in a position to begin doing precisely that. Mapping the dynamics of the unconscious brought him to the threshold of great things, giving him something new and consequential to say on all the questions that had preoccupied the West since at least Plato's time. At the end of the first decade of the twentieth century, Sigmund Freud was looking forward to life, and more life, with an intensity that not all men of fifty-three can muster.

In the fall of 1909, when Hitler was walking confused and lonely through Vienna, Freud had recently returned from a triumphal visit to the United States. Accompanied by his closest disciples, Carl Jung, Sándor Ferenczi, and Ernest Jones, he'd spent a week in New York touring the city, then gone off to Worcester, Massachusetts. There, at Clark University, he gave a celebrated set of talks, which were attended by, among others, America's preeminent philosopher and psychologist, William James, and by Emma Goldman—the formidable anarchist intellectual, who found herself in agreement with a good deal of what Freud had to say. Freud even received an honorary degree at Clark. Thinking back to the trip, he would write: "In Europe I felt as though I were despised; but over there I found myself received by the foremost men as an equal. It seemed like the realization of some incredible daydream." Freud returned from America with his confidence and his energies redoubled, ready to do what he believed would be great work.

The work that Freud did do, following the American sojourn, went in an unexpected direction. Up until 1909, Freud, to speak broadly, had been fascinated with the dynamics of desire. He wanted to know how the unconscious, the seat and source of desire, worked and in particular how it expressed itself in neuroses and dreams and in works of art. It was during this period that Freud was inclined to see erotic urges—and also, less consequentially, aggressive drives—at the root of human behavior. But as time went on, Freud became more and more preoccupied with the issue of authority, and with the agency that he thought of as the center of authority in the human psyche, the superego, or over-I.

In a few years, Freud would begin to write a sequence of books and essays that focused on authority that had become toxic, authority gone bad. He would become preoccupied with tyranny—with the human hunger for power and the human desire to be dominated. In *Group Psychology and the Analysis of the Ego, Totem and Taboo, The Future of an Illusion,* and many other works, Freud would reflect on what makes human beings respond to tyrants—not just obey them, but honor and love them. He would, in a certain sense, soon start to think in depth about the man that the young Adolf Hitler, his fellow resident of Vienna in 1909, would become, and also about all the tyrants who have followed Hitler through the twentieth century and on into the twenty-first.

If Hitler and Freud passed each other on the street on an afternoon during the cold late autumn of 1909, what would each of them have seen? In Hitler, Freud would have seen a rank denizen of the crowd, a street rat. (Freud was no populist.) But he probably would have felt sorry for the unfortunate man as well. For his part, Hitler would have seen a Viennese burgher (he despised the upper middle class) and probably would have recognized Freud as a Jew. Hitler would have drawn back in shame at his threadbare overcoat and his broken-down shoes. If things were bad enough, he might have extended a hand to beg. Whether Freud gave or not—he could well have; he was generally good-hearted—would have made little difference; the encounter would still have left the young Adolf Hitler seething.

*   *   *

But time passed and the world changed. Almost three decades later, in 1938, the former street rat was the chancellor of Germany and one of the most powerful men in the world. In 1933 he had been elected—no coup was involved (though some devious machinations were)—to the most important office in his nation. Twenty-five years after his desperate period in Vienna, Adolf Hitler achieved the ascendancy he dreamed about when he was giving his speeches to the disbelieving crowd at the men's shelter.

During the First World War Hitler had come into his own. He became a dispatch runner in the German army, serving with stunning bravery and twice winning the Iron Cross. After the war, he joined a small political party in Munich—at the beginning there had been only a handful of members—and he turned it into a powerful alliance. He attempted a coup in 1923, failed, and was sentenced to prison. While he was there, he wrote *Mein Kampf,* where he described his past life and laid down his program for Germany's future. There followed a decade of astonishing work, campaigning, speaking, brawling, writing, forming and destroying alliances, until, at the end of it, Adolf Hitler was the preeminent man in Germany. Of course he had further ambitions: he wanted the world. But in 1938, Adolf Hitler desired one thing above all others, and that was Austria.

Soon Hitler would be headed again to Vienna, the city where he had been so badly abused and humiliated, but this time he would not be coming with a sketchbook and a pittance in his pocket. He would arrive instead with thousands of troops at his back. On the first page of *Mein Kampf,* Hitler had announced that Austria must be made part of the German nation, and now that he was in power, he was determined to bring this event to pass. Even in middle age, after he became chancellor, Hitler recalled time and again how he had spent the worst years of his life in Vienna. He said that he had come to the city as a mother's boy, and that Vienna had made him hard. Sometimes he joked with his intimates about how satisfying it would be to destroy the entire city and to start again from scratch.

Waiting for Hitler in Vienna in that winter of 1938 was an old and desperately ill Sigmund Freud—as well as a hundred and seventy-five thousand other racial enemies. The Nazis hated Freud with a particular vehemence. When they burned his books at their outdoor rallies in Germany in 1933, the presiding officer had shouted out an indictment: "Against the soul-destroying glorification of the instinctual life," he cried, "for the nobility of the human soul! I consign to the flames the writings of Sigmund Freud." Freud, hearing the news about the book burning, remarked, "What progress we are making. In the Middle Ages they would have burnt me; nowadays they are content with burning my books." Five years later, the Nazis who were preparing to invade Austria, and the ones who lived there themselves—there were many—might not be content with merely the burning of books.

Sigmund Freud did not appear to be ready for strife of any sort. He was eighty-one years old and he seemed smaller than his modest height; he was bent and brittle and precariously thin. His beard had gone completely white, and was cropped close to his cheeks; he wore black-framed oval glasses that gave him an owlish appearance. His skin, which was blanched and seemed thin as rice paper, stretched taut against his face. He could no longer speak with force and clarity because of the prosthesis implanted in his jaw to replace the teeth and bone that had been removed during the many operations for his cancer. His eyes, as almost everyone who knew him during those days attested, remained potent: at times, Freud did not stare at things, so much as through them to the other side. Overall, his presence was unnerving: by 1938, deep into old age, Freud looked like a dark fairy-tale version of Death himself.

Adolf Hitler's Austrian aggression—and the drama that composed the last two years of Sigmund Freud's life—began when Hitler summoned Kurt von Schuschnigg, Austria's chancellor, to his compound at Berchtesgaden. (Now the onetime street rat had the leaders of nations at his beck and call.) An introverted, scholarly man who wore rimless glasses and chain-smoked, Schuschnigg was no match for the führer. Hitler issued ultimatums. He demanded that Austria legalize the Nazi Party; he demanded that Nazis be installed in the government; he demanded a military treaty between the two nations. He also required that Austria hold a plebiscite so its citizens could vote on unification with the grand German nation. Schuschnigg, nervous, badly in need of a cigarette, yet aware that no one, under any conditions, smoked in the presence of the führer, had not gone to Germany expecting an easy interview. (Before leaving, he remarked that he should be bringing a psychiatrist along to help him contend with Hitler.) Still Schuschnigg was shocked by what he heard.

"You don't seriously believe that you can stop me or even delay me for half an hour, do you?" the führer asked. "Perhaps you will wake up one morning in Vienna to find us there—just like a spring storm. And then you'll see something. I would very much like to save Austria from such a fate, because such an action would mean blood."

Hitler had been brooding on Austria for some time and he had a great deal to impart to Schuschnigg. "The whole history of Austria," Hitler told the chancellor during the meeting, "is just one uninterrupted act of high treason. That was so in the past and is no better today." Schuschnigg was so anxious that he refrained from reminding Hitler that he himself had been born in Austria. The führer went on, his rage expanding: "And I can tell you right now, Herr Schuschnigg, that I am absolutely determined to make an end of all this. The German Reich is one of the great powers and nobody will raise his voice if it settles its border problems."

"I have a historic mission," Hitler said, "and this mission I will fulfill because Providence has destined me to do so. I thoroughly believe in this mission; it is my life . . . Look around you in Germany today, Herr Schuschnigg, and you will find that there is but one will." Hitler told the Austrian chancellor that his triumph was inevitable: "I have made the greatest achievement in the history of Germany, greater than any other German." When Schuschnigg informed Hitler that France and

England would not stand by and allow him to absorb Austria, the führer laughed.

Over the past decade, Hitler had nearly consolidated his power over the German people; he had done away with his party enemies in a quick, bloody purge, the Night of the Long Knives (Freud, hearing the news of the purge, expressed a wish that the Nazis might have killed each other off to the last man: that was just an hors d'oeuvre, he said, where is the main course?); Hitler had earned the friendship of Mussolini, the only national leader that he respected; he had become certain that the democracies were weak, irresolute, and would not risk war against him. Now he could look out to the world at large with an unlimited sense of possibility. In vigorous middle age, Hitler had never felt so potent, so much a man of destiny.

Freud's own situation was much more precarious. On January 22, he had been forced to undergo yet another operation for the cancer of the jaw that had been tormenting him for fifteen years. This time the tumor was hard to reach, because it was close to Freud's eye socket, so his surgeon, Hans Pichler, had to create a special implement to get at it. Freud spent two days in the sanatorium, and then, still in great pain, made his way home to rest. Freud knew that the cancer was the result of his incessant cigar smoking, and he had been told many times to stop, but he wouldn't. He loved cigars too much: at the height of his consumption, he smoked twenty a day. When things were especially bad, he sometimes used a clothespin to open his frozen, aching jaw so as to wedge one more into his mouth.

The January operation was especially brutal, and it was followed by another, on February 19, a few days after Hitler's meeting with Schuschnigg. In this operation, Pichler cut out a suspect wart in the cancerous region, and fortunately, the bioposy on the new growth was negative. This operation was less painful than the previous one, but the patient was eighty-one years old, and physically at least, he was very frail. It wasn't at all clear how many more such ordeals Freud could take.

Freud left the clinic and spent his time resting and recuperating at Berggasse 19, the apartment where he had been living for fifty years and that he now shared with his wife, Martha; her sister, Aunt Minna; and Anna, the Freuds' daughter. Here Freud had developed his psychoanalytical practice, raised his six children, and written the books and papers that made him known throughout the West.

Berggasse—literally Hill Street—deserves its name; it's a frequently steep thoroughfare that begins at the Tandelmarkt, Vienna's flea market, and runs to the Votivkirche, a modern Gothic cathedral. By Viennese standards, Freud lived in a respectable, though not truly distinguished, neighborhood. Berggasse 19 was built in the 1870s; the lower part of the building is Renaissance style, the upper features classical revival work. Downstairs to the left of the apartment house was Siegmund Kornmehl's butcher shop, on the right a food cooperative, the Ersten Wiener Consum-Vereines. The Freud family lived on the mezzanine, the second floor of the building.

Though from the outside it looked conventional enough, the

Freuds' apartment at Berggasse 19 was actually a place like none other in Vienna, and in fact like none other in the world. In the back of the dwelling, Freud had fashioned himself a private kingdom of two rooms, and it was here that he retired during the bad days in February and early March, after the two operations, to nurse his aching jaw, to gather his powers, and to see what Adolf Hitler would do.

Throughout his life, Freud had been a ferocious worker, able to push on through intense pain, but now he was spending much of his time lying down on the couch that his patients used when they came in for analysis. This was the famous divan that he had sat at the foot of during so many sessions over so many years, out of sight of his patients—"I cannot put up with being stared at . . . for eight hours a day (or more)," he once said—smoking his cigars, keeping himself in a state of evenly suspended attention, and listening, listening. The couch, Freud ruefully said, was "meant for others," but these days he needed it himself.

Yet however weak and uncertain Freud may have appeared in those hard days in March of 1938, however much he may seem to have declined from the confident, ambitious figure who strolled through the streets of Vienna in 1909, he was still Sigmund Freud, and that meant a number of things. It meant that he was an extremely rebellious and passionate man who would say things, write things, and even sometimes do things that his contemporaries found shocking. He was self-reliant and daring and, when it came to action, ultimately consulted no one but himself.

But as rebellious as Freud could be—and delighted in being—he was also a man who was attracted to convention.

Freud was interested in conventional success, in money, in fame, in having a sterling reputation, in maintaining an impeccable bourgeois household. (There were few apartments more bland than Berggasse 19—until one reached Freud's inner sanctum.) He wanted to fit in and he wanted to succeed, even as he was committed to a mode of thought that was genuinely revolutionary.

Freud's passion was manifest time after time in his life. When he fell in love with his future wife, Martha Bernays, he fell furiously in love. He wrote her wildly adoring letters; he fumed with jealousy. Somewhat in the mode of a medieval troubadour, he dreamed up an image of Martha that was exotic, erotically rich, complex—and at some variance with the sweet, decent young woman he actually married. The two were apart for much of their long engagement, and in his letters Freud was a writer of romantic fiction par excellence. "Martha is mine," he cried to her in one letter, "the sweet girl of whom everyone speaks with admiration, who despite all my resistance captivated my heart at our first meeting, the girl I feared to court and who came toward me with high-minded confidence, who strengthened the faith in my own value and gave me new hope and energy to work when I needed it most."

Freud was also prone to fall for men. His involvements with his mentors, men like Wilhelm Fliess and Josef Breuer, have a lover's intensity, and his eventual breaks with them have the drama of erotic terminations. He brought the same passion to his relations with his disciples. Jung, whom he hoped would inherit his role as the head of the psychoanalytical movement— Freud liked to refer to him as the "crown prince"—was genuinely beloved by Freud. When they quarreled and eventually went separate ways, Freud's world shuddered.

He was a similarly passionate thinker: it sometimes appears that there was nothing that crossed his mind that he would not write down and publish. It's not only that Freud declared the existence of the Oedipal complex, shocking the world with the view that all children want to have sex with their mothers and do away with their fathers; not only that he believed that infants were sexually alert and sexually responsive beings. These ideas were central to Freud's vision of human life: he could hardly suppress them. But at times expanding the broad wings of his imagination, Freud seemed incapable of holding anything back.

How did mankind gain control over fire? Freud believed that he knew. In prehistoric times, fire came to earth through lightning storms. A branch would flame up and drop to the ground. But generally, when men saw this happen, they would approach the flames and urinate on them until they went out. This was, according to Freud, a source of great pleasure. "The legends that we possess," he said, "leave no doubt about the originally phallic view taken of tongues of flame as they shoot upwards. Putting out fire by micturating—a theme to which modern giants, Gulliver in Lilliput and Rabelais's Gargantua, still hark back—was therefore a kind of sexual act with a male, an enjoyment of sexual potency in a homosexual competition." At some point, a man capable of instinctual renunciation came along and was able to refrain from dousing the flames. He brought the fire back to his cave and experimented with it, finding that he could use it for heat and for cooking. Thus did mankind conquer fire. This fable—a remarkable twist on the

Prometheus story—occurs not in a letter or a conversation, but as a footnote in what is perhaps Freud's best-composed book, *Civilization and Its Discontents.* Why did Freud write such a thing? Because he thought it was true—and what Freud thought to be true, he wrote and published, period.

Time after time in his work, Freud changed course, revised himself, came up with ideas stranger and more off-putting (and often more brilliantly illuminating) than the strange, off-putting ideas of his already in place. At one point he decided, based on very thin evidence—assuming there was any evidence at all— that something called the "Death Drive" is a force in all organic life. All beings, Freud declared, have an urge to return to an earlier state of things, to seek destruction and decomposition and to do so after their own fashion. "The aim of all life," Freud famously declared, "is death." Looking around him and pondering as deeply as possible, Freud simply concluded that this was true, and rather than suppress the idea, he did all he could to develop it—and damn the consequences for his reputation and the reputation of psychoanalysis. Until the end of his life, the Death Drive was for Freud an open hypothesis: from his point of view, he simply ran out of time to confirm it.

Yet the same Sigmund Freud, being asked if he raised his children according to the tenets of psychoanalysis, simply grunted and replied that he raised his children as children— that is, pretty much according to convention—and that was all there was to it. Freud lived his whole life through as a conventional bourgeois: he was well dressed at all times; his hair and beard were always trimmed; he paid his debts and got places on time. While to many he was the great advocate of

Eros, his own erotic life seems to have been almost entirely conventional. Speculations to the effect that Freud had a love affair with his sister-in-law, Minna Bernays, remain just that—speculations.

Then there was the matter of Freud's intellectual identity. He fought to attain the rank of Professor, not only because it would help him to earn more, but because it added to his quotient of respectability. Though on some level Freud surely knew that the kinds of books and essays he was writing were without any obvious precedent and that in many ways they were closer to literature than to anything else—"the drives," he once said, "are our mythology"—he went on insisting that he was a scientist and demanded for psychoanalysis all the prestige that science possessed. He sought prizes and honors—though he sometimes claimed not to—and he quietly cherished them when they came his way. Though Freud declared time and again that he hated to be photographed, it sometimes seems that there were times in his life when he did little but. In his photos, Freud seems to be trying to look ever more wise, stable, authoritative, and commanding.

Freud is at his best when his two potent drives, the drive to rebellion and the drive to logic and respectability, animate each other. The result then is thinking that is rigorously presented, is well argued, and takes account of myriad objections, but that is also astonishing in its originality. Among such performances are books like *Civilization and Its Discontents*, *The Ego and the Id*, *Group Psychology and the Analysis of the Ego*, *Totem and Taboo*, *Three Essays on the Theory of Sexuality*, *The Interpretation of Dreams*, and *Beyond the Pleasure Principle*. There are also major essays in this mode, pieces like "On Narcissism," "Mourning and Melancholia," "Analysis Terminable and Interminable," "Humour," "The Uncanny," and the best of the articles on therapy and technique that Freud wrote to guide future analysts. Here Freud is not only as bold in his conceptions as any poet, but clear, shrewd, and impressively self-critical.

From at least the time he set out on his professional road, in his twenties, Freud was both a cannily and rigorously conventional man and something on the order of a visionary. The tendencies shifted all the time—sometimes one dominated, sometimes the other, and sometimes they entered a rich synergy. But Freud's intellect was always intense and inventive. Sigmund Freud at eighty-one and Sigmund Freud at thirty-one were, despite appearances, not drastically different beings, at least internally. Close to the end of his life, William Blake, whose poetry anticipates Freud's thinking in certain ways, observed in a letter that he has been near death and has returned "very weak & an Old Man feeble & tottering, but not in Spirit & Life not in The Real Man The Imagination which Liveth for Ever. In that I am stronger & stronger as this Foolish Body decays." In 1938, Freud was surely feeble enough in body, but The Real Man in him was still alive.

On February 20, the day after Freud's operation, Hitler addressed the German Reichstag on the Austrian problem and the speech was broadcast not only in Germany but in

Austria as well. The many concessions he had compelled Schuschnigg to make at Berchtesgaden would not be enough, Hitler declared. Austria was continuing to mistreat its German citizens: it was "intolerable," the führer declared, "for a self-conscious world power to know that at its side are co-racials who are subjected to continuous suffering because of their sympathy and unity with the whole German race and its ideology." The speech went on for hours, with Hitler rising to a frenzy of rage against Germany's oppressors. After the speech, Austrian Nazis began to gather in the streets of Vienna and to chant "Sieg Heil! Sieg Heil! Heil Hitler! Heil Hitler!" G. E. R. Gedye, a newspaper correspondent, described the sound coming from the German legation. "As one first caught it in the distance it was just a rhythmic throb, like the beating of a feverish pulse, which as one approached seemed to change into the inarticulate but disciplined cawing of some militarized rookery—'A-a-a-ah—Aaah! A-a-a-a-h—Aah–A-a-a-ah—Aah!,' and finally into audible words." Soon the brownshirts were in the streets and rioting.

On the day of Hitler's speech, Freud's daughter Anna wrote a letter to Ernest Jones, Freud's most trusted disciple next to Anna herself, sizing up the situation. "There was an atmosphere of panic in Vienna," she said, "which has now calmed down a little. We have not joined in the panic. It is too early, one can not yet fully assess the consequences of what has happened. For the time being everything is as it was. It is perhaps easier for us than for others who are more mobile, we do not need to consider many decisions since for us hardly any come into consideration." What Anna Freud meant was that her father was too old and too sick to try to escape, and that in any event, he would probably never consent to leave Vienna.

Things had been turbulent in Vienna before, and Freud had never contemplated leaving. This was not the first Nazi threat to the city, and in fact, ever since 1918, with the end of the First World War and the collapse of the Austro-Hungarian Empire, Vienna's situation had been precarious. There was massive inflation in the 1920s, then deflation, followed by the great economic depression of the 1930s. There had been a socialist uprising in the working-class districts of Vienna in 1934, which had been brutally suppressed, with the leaders barely escaping through Vienna's famed sewer system. All through the 1930s, the once small Austrian Nazi Party grew. In July 1933, the Christian Socialist chancellor Engelbert Dollfuss outlawed it, but by then, the party, made up of tradesmen, small shop-keepers, veterans, recent university graduates, and many po-licemen, counted seventy thousand members. The Nazis were bound together by anti-Semitism (as virulent as any to be found in Germany), anti-clericalism, anti-Catholicism, and the desire for unification with Germany. During the months after it was banned, the party picked up twenty thousand new members.

In the summer of 1934, with Hitler now chancellor of Germany, a small group of Nazi SS men dressed themselves in Austrian army uniforms and invaded the Chancellery. There they caught Chancellor Dollfuss attempting to escape through a side door, shot and killed him. They took over the radio station and announced to the country that the government had resigned. But there were potent divisions in the Austrian Nazi

Party at the time—it was just after the Night of the Long Knives—and most Nazis refused to join in the putsch. Hitler, who had approved the attempt, was compelled to back off and disown it. Soon afterward, Dollfuss's killers were hanged in the yard of the Vienna regional court, and some of the other plotters went to jail. For a while, Nazi activity in Vienna quieted. But by 1938 the Austrian Nazi Party was growing stronger again. The Nazis wore their swastika pins on the inside of their lapels, ready to turn them out at the right moment; they greeted each other with "Heil Hitler," and sometimes on the street, they exchanged the salute.

Yet even now, with the situation worsening, Anna Freud was quite right to suggest that her father would not consent to leave, for Sigmund Freud loved—and despised—the city a great deal. Vienna was where Freud had lived for nearly all his life and where he had, against no little resistance, done his work. The resistance in Vienna to Freud was twofold: he had difficulties because he was a Jew and difficulties because of his ideas. From the time that Freud went into medicine and biological research, almost everyone around him recognized his vast talents. Nonetheless his advancement through the professional ranks was slow. It took Freud a long time to secure the title that he wanted—the title of "Professor"—to attract patients, and to generate a solid income. This had no little to do with the fact that Freud was a Jew and a Jew who, irreligious as he was, had no inclination to deny his origins. In fact, he thrust them forward aggressively.

When Freud was very young, his father told him a story about how he had gone for a walk one Saturday, decked out in a new fur hat. Along came a Christian, who with a single blow knocked the cap off Jacob Freud's head and into the mud. "Jew! get off the pavement," the Christian hollered. "And what did you do?" Freud asked. He wanted to hear about how his dear papa stood up to the bigot and put him in his place. But that is not what Jacob told him. "I went into the roadway and picked up my cap." The young Freud—he couldn't have been more than ten or twelve—was outraged. "This struck me as unheroic conduct on the part of the big strong man who was holding the little boy by the hand," Freud reflected years later. "I contrasted this situation with another which fitted my feelings better: the scene in which Hannibal's father, Hamilcar Barca, made his boy swear before the household altar to take vengeance on the Romans." From then on, Hannibal had a major place in Freud's imaginative life. Freud resolved that he would never be humiliated by the bigots who surrounded him and his family in Vienna. In the future he would struggle with the gentiles when he had to, and never step aside.

But it wasn't only Freud's Jewish identity that created trouble for him; his ideas themselves, once they began to attract attention, caused scandals. When Freud published his book on the theory of sexuality, with its insistence that infants lived thriving erotic lives (they could devolve into "polymorphous perverts," he believed), respectable people crossed the street in order to avoid him. Freud's response was not only to keep the book in print, but also to update it and revise it regularly, a distinction he conferred only on texts that mattered a great deal to him, such as his first major book, *The Interpretation of Dreams.*

But Freud, if never exactly happy in Vienna (Freud did not put much of a premium on happiness per se), nonetheless knew that it provided him one of the things he most needed, which was productive conflict. Like certain contentious, passionate poets, such as Milton, whom Freud read and admired, and Blake, whom Freud would have admired had he read, Freud understood that he did his best work when he had opposition in front of him. And work was to Freud the ultimate goal: he measured every day by how much and how well he produced. He once remarked that for all to go well, he needed to have a close friend to confide in and a spirited enemy to oppose. "My emotional life has always insisted that I should have an intimate friend and a hated enemy," Freud said. "I have always been able to provide myself afresh with both." In fact, Freud's close friends often obligingly transformed themselves—or were transformed by Freud—into inspiring enemies. But Freud thrived against collective opposition too. He loved good intellectual fights and he believed that he owed his power to sustain those fights and use them to generate more work to his Jewish background. Jews, he said, are accustomed to being in opposition; it's a part of the legacy. "It was only to my Jewish nature," he wrote once, "that I owed the two qualities that have become indispensable to me throughout my difficult life. Because I was a Jew I found myself free of many prejudices which restrict others in the use of the intellect: as a Jew I was prepared to be in the opposition."

Yet as a mental warrior, Freud was not usually white-lipped, vindictive, or bitter. He proceeded with high spirits, possessed by an intellectual form of what heroic cultures call "battle joy." "I am not really a man of science," he wrote once, "not an observer, not an experimenter, and not a thinker. I am nothing but by temperament a *conquistador*—an adventurer, if you want to translate the word—with the curiosity, the boldness, and the tenacity that belong to that type of being. Such people are apt to be treasured if they succeed, if they have really discovered something; otherwise they are thrown aside. And that is not altogether unjust."

Freud found in Vienna what he needed: many spirited opponents, some people open-minded enough to come to him when no other doctor could help, and a small minority of students, and then disciples, who were truly interested in his ideas. But the opposition he was looking at in the winter of 1938 threatened far more than denying him the professional standing that was his due, denouncing his ideas, or ruining his reputation.

On March 9, the mild Kurt von Schuschnigg defied Adolf Hitler. During the conference at Berchtesgaden, when Hitler had delivered his threat of invasion, he demanded that Austria hold a plebiscite so the Austrian people could decide whether or not they wanted to unite with Germany. Hitler was sure he would win and had reason to be, for the Austrian Nazi Party was gaining strength with each passing month.

After a couple of weeks' lull, Schuschnigg gave a speech calling for the referendum to be held almost immediately—on Sunday, March 13. He was doing exactly what Hitler demanded, but with a twist: citizens had to be at least twenty-four years old to vote in Schuschnigg's referendum. The Austrian Nazis were young: the National Socialists were the party of choice for anyone who wanted to rise in the world and be part of an imperial nation. Without young people voting, the chances were that the plebiscite would go in favor of Austrian independence. Holding the vote soon would also ensure that Hitler and Goebbels didn't have the time to initiate a lavish propaganda campaign. In the speech on March 9, Schuschnigg, decked out in the traditional Austrian gray jacket and green waistcoat, looked out at his audience and asked, "Are you in favor of a free and German, independent and social, a Christian and united Austria?" The crowd of twenty thousand roared assent. Schuschnigg finished the speech with the words of the Austrian hero Andreas Hofer, calling on his countrymen to resist Napoleon. "Men—the hour has struck!" For Hitler, this was not to be borne.

But Hitler was now concerned not only with the Austrian nationalists but also with Mussolini, who was, supposedly, Austria's protector. Hitler wrote to him immediately, requesting the right to do what he liked about his former home country: "In my responsibility as Führer and Chancellor of the German Reich and likewise as a son of the soil . . . I am now determined to restore law and order in my homeland and enable the people to decide their own fate according to their judgment in an unmistakable, clear and open manner." Hitler made various professions of fealty to Il Duce, then dispatched Prince Philip of Hesse to deliver the letter as quickly as possible. The prince boarded a plane to Italy carrying the critical message, along with a basket of plants for his garden in Rome.

In Vienna, Schuschnigg's speech provoked action: on Thursday afternoon, trucks equipped with speakers rolled through the streets, announcing the plebiscite and urging people to vote "Ja" on Sunday. Austrian patriots ranged all over Vienna, chanting, "Heil Schuschnigg!" "Heil Liberty!" and "Sunday is polling day: We vote Ja!" For a while, it seemed as though Austria might actually be able to stand alone against Germany. By evening, though, the Nazis were on the streets too. They walked four abreast through the center of Vienna, sounding their war cry: "One People! One Nation! One Leader!" At first the Austrian patriots looked on benignly: they outnumbered the Nazis at least three to one. But then scuffles began and the police jumped in on the side of the Nazis and started beating the nationalists. Before long, the streets belonged to the storm troopers.

Early Friday morning, Hitler, still having heard nothing from Mussolini, made his decision: he issued invasion plans to his staff. "If other measures prove unsuccessful," he said, "I intend to invade Austria with armed forces in order to establish constitutional conditions and to prevent further outrages against the pro-German population." At five thirty that morning, Schuschnigg received a phone call letting him know that the Germans had closed their border with Austria; soon the chancellor discovered that German troops were being mobilized in Munich. At ten o'clock, demands came to Schuschnigg from

Berlin: he must resign his office immediately and turn it over to a member of the Nazi Party, and he must postpone the plebiscite for at least two weeks.

If he did not do so, the Germans would "act accordingly." Backed to the wall, Schuschnigg sent a telegram pleading for help to the British prime minister, Neville Chamberlain, who, as chance had it, was at a lunch on Downing Street in honor of the German ambassador, Joachim von Ribbentrop. Confronted with the reports from Vienna, Ribbentrop lied. He said that he knew nothing about a crisis in Austria and said that the reports might well be mistaken. It did not take Chamberlain long to decide what it was that he and England would do: nothing. He had Lord Halifax send a cable off to Schuschnigg, telling him as much. "His Majesty's government cannot take responsibility," the communiqué began. Ribbentrop stayed late into the afternoon, satisfied that things at home were going well. Winston Churchill, who was present at the lunch too, recalls how "the Ribbentrops lingered on, so that most of us made our excuses and our way home. Eventually I suppose they left." But then Churchill adds a sentence: "That was the last time I saw Herr von Ribbentrop before he was hanged."

With no help coming from England, France, or anywhere else, it became clear to Schuschnigg that there was nothing he could do.

Shortly after Schuschnigg's March 9 speech, help came Freud's way from a most unexpected source, the United States of

America. America: there was no nation that Sigmund Freud disliked more. Despite his having been so well treated there when he visited in 1909, and despite the early success psychoanalysis enjoyed in the United States, Freud never ceased to detest the country. To him, America represented a social catastrophe nearly as dire as the one embodied by the Nazis gathering along Austria's border. Virtually everything he knew—or thought he knew—about the United States irritated Sigmund Freud.

Americans, first off, were obsessed by money. Everyone in America, Freud believed, was dully materialistic, without cultivation, without subtlety, without the capacity to enjoy life's higher pleasures. The word "dollars" shows up in almost all of Freud's denunciations of the United States. In America, they compete with each other bitterly and worship the almighty dollar, and that alone, Freud said, time after time. They're all afflicted with a hideous disease: "dollaria." As he put it in a letter to Ernest Jones: "The Americans are really 'too bad.' . . . Competition is much more pungent with them, not succeeding means civil death to every one and they have no private resources apart from their profession, no hobby, games, love, or other interests of a cultured person. And success means money. Can an American live in opposition to the public opinion as we are prepared to do?" It is an unfortunate fact, but nonetheless true: when Freud fulminates about American obsessions with wealth, he can sound uncomfortably like an anti-Semite grousing about Jewish money-hunger. Yet no such awareness ever stemmed Freud's feelings about American dollaria.

Freud was also convinced that Americans were prudes. He believed that their interests in moneymaking absorbed the libido that they could have invested in sensuous pleasure. All their energy was devoted to the pursuit of cash; for the pursuit of pleasure, nothing was left. Freud conceived of psychoanalysis as a way to relax what he called "civilized sexual morality," which expected far too much repression from individuals. Americans, in Freud's understanding, loved damming up their erotic energies, the better to rechannel them for the pursuit of prosperity. Freud even castigated American love affairs, rare occurrences that they presumably were, for being slight and fleeting. Why did they lack passionate depth? Because, presumably, Americans were so keyed to the present that when they fell in love, if you could call it that, they didn't activate the old parental prototypes—there was nothing deeply Oedipal, that is, ambivalent, tormented, strange—about their erotic encounters.

But what most disturbed Freud about America was its politics. Americans suffered from what Freud liked to call the "psychological poverty of groups." Much like de Tocqueville, but with far less sympathy, Freud saw America as a nation where the group tended to rule over, and often to crush, the individual. Not only did America always teeter close to mob rule; it was doomed to mediocrity because the lowest common denominator would always prevail. In America, there was no room for true leaders. The crowd, mesmerized by democratic propaganda, believed that it was always in the right. The people never needed to change or develop their vision of life. "My suspicion of America," Freud said, "is unconquerable."

When associates pointed out to Freud, as they often did, that no nation outside of Germany and Austria was more hospitable to psychoanalysis than America, Freud's inevitable reply was that Americans had no idea what psychoanalysis was actually about. "We are bringing them the plague," Freud purportedly said when he and Jung and Ferenczi disembarked in New York in 1909. "We're bringing them the plague, and they don't even know it."

Yet when the Nazis threatened Vienna, Americans rushed forward to help Freud. On March 10, Freud had a visit from John Wiley, the chargé d'affaires at the American Embassy in Vienna. Wiley, a man of the world, never seen without his extralong cigarette holder, inquired about Freud's welfare, asked about the rest of the family, and made it clear that the United States would do all it could to protect them. Wiley was a close colleague of William Bullitt, who was then the American ambassador to France, and Bullitt considered himself to be a particular friend of Freud's. Bullitt was a charming, affable man from a wealthy Philadelphia Main Line family; there was no one in the diplomatic world he didn't know. Bullitt had worked for a while with Woodrow Wilson, and then broken with the president over the Versailles Treaty. After the war, he made himself notorious by criticizing Wilson and the treaty to the Senate Foreign Relations Committee.

Bullitt had come to Freud in the mid-1920s, attempting to find a cure for what he took to be his self-destructive behavior. (Testifying against the president to the Senate probably began to look like precisely that in retrospect.) Then Bullitt reappeared at Freud's doorstep in 1930, with an idea for a project. He wanted to collaborate on a book about Woodrow Wilson, a psychological study, and Freud, surprisingly, agreed. Freud was constantly being approached with schemes like this, and they tended to come from America. The publisher of the *Chicago Tribune* offered Freud twenty-five thousand dollars to travel to Chicago to psychoanalyze the killers Leopold and Loeb. The producer Samuel Goldwyn claimed that he was ready to give Freud a hundred thousand dollars to come to Hollywood and collaborate on making movies. After all, Goldwyn observed, who knows more about laughter and love—the staples of good movies—than Sigmund Freud? To both offers, Freud said no: he almost always turned such opportunities down, despite the fact that he was usually short of money. Freud had been very taken with Bullitt, though, and agreed to the collaboration; and in fact the Wilson book was, in time, published. Now Bullitt was going to do all he could for the man he so admired. Largely because of Bullitt, Freud would soon have the sympathetic attention of the president of the rogue republic himself, Franklin Delano Roosevelt.

The day after Wiley's visit, Friday, March 11, 1938, Sigmund Freud did something that he disliked: he listened to the radio. His son Martin Freud says that this was the only occasion that he could recall his father doing so. What Freud heard that evening was the voice of Kurt von Schuschnigg, but now Schuschnigg's defiance was gone. The chancellor was canceling the plebiscite on Austrian independence and resigning from office. In the hopes of avoiding slaughter, Schuschnigg encouraged the Austrian army not to fight back when the German troops came rolling across the border, as they now seemed certain to do. "We have yielded to force," the chancellor said. "Because under no circumstances, not even in this supreme hour, do we intend that German blood shall be spilt, we have instructed our army to retreat without offering any resistance." Schuschnigg's final words to the country were grieving: "Thus I take leave of the Austrian nation with a German farewell which also expresses my heartfelt wish: God save Austria!"

As soon as the speech was over, Vienna came alive again with chants of "One People, One Nation, One Leader!" as well as cries of "Death to the Jews!" William Shirer, the American reporter, saw young men heave paving blocks through the windows of Jewish shops. The crowds egged them on and roared with pleasure as the windows shattered and the glass dropped like great ice chunks into the street.

"As I crossed the Graben," G. E. R. Gedye recalls, "the Brown flood was sweeping through the streets. It was an indescribable witches' Sabbath—storm-troopers, lots of them barely out of the schoolroom, with cartridge-belts and carbines, the only other evidence of authority being Swastika brassards, were marching side by side with police turncoats, men and women shrieking or crying hysterically the name of their leader, embracing the police and dragging them along in the swirling stream of humanity, motor-lorries filled with storm-troopers clutching their long-concealed weapons, hooting furiously, trying to make themselves heard above the din, men and women leaping, shouting and dancing in the light of the smoking torches which soon began to make their appearance, the air filled with a pandemonium of sound in which intermingled screams of: Down with the Jews! Heil Hitler! Heil Hitler! Sieg Heil! Perish the Jews! Hang Schuschnigg!"

Nazis began to mobilize all over Austria. An SS group took control of the headquarters of the Tyrolese provincial government. In Linz, not far from the führer's birthplace, twenty thousand people gathered to cheer the news that Schuschnigg was gone. The Nazi high command in Berlin told their colleagues, newly installed in the Austrian government, that it was time to make a formal request for Germany to "step in and restore order"—the order that Germany was destroying. By ten past nine that evening, the communiqué asking for German assistance was out. At ten forty-five, Prince Philip of Hesse, who had gone to Italy in Hitler's behalf, phoned the führer to let him know that all was in order and that Il Duce endorsed the invasion. "Please tell Mussolini I will never forget him for this," Hitler said, "Never, never, never, whatever happens."

At five thirty the next morning, Saturday, March 12, 1938, the German troops that had gathered along the border in Bavaria crossed over into Austria with no opposition. The Annexation—the Anschluss—had begun.

Later that Saturday, Freud made a two-word entry in his journal, "Finis Austria": the end of Austria. That morning, Freud's paper, *Neue Freie Presse*, announced that Arthur Seyss-Inquart, a "moderate" Austrian Nazi, was now in control of the government. But it was the evening's paper that enraged Freud. Martin, Freud's son, remembered how his father gently took the paper from the maid and read through the headlines. He sat for a while, pondering. Then the old man crumpled it all up in a ball and hurled it across the room. Freud was, at home as he was abroad in the world, an extremely self-contained man who did not readily show emotion. Martin had never seen his father act this way. No one dared ask Freud a question; no one dared to speak. After a while Martin softly crossed the room, picked up the sheets, unfolded them, and read. In the paper was Hitler's proclamation justifying the invasion; it ended with the words "Long Live National Socialist Germany-Austria!"

Freud may have been enraged at what was happening in Austria, but he was not entirely unprepared for it. Writing to his son Ernst in 1934, the year after Hitler came to power, Freud said, "The future is uncertain: either Austrian fascism or the swastika. . . . Our attitude to the two political possibilities for Austria's future can only be summed up in Mercutio's line in *Romeo and Juliet*: 'A plague on both your houses.'" By 1936, things looked, if possible, more dire to Freud: "Austria seems bent on becoming National Socialist," he wrote to Arnold Zweig. "Fate seems to be conspiring with that gang. With ever less regret do I wait for the curtain to fall on me."

In 1937, a year before Hitler made his move on Austria, Freud felt nearly certain how things would go. "Our political situation seems to become more and more gloomy," he told Ernest Jones. "The invasion of the Nazis can probably not be checked; the consequences are disastrous for analysis as well. The only hope remaining is that one will not live to see it oneself. The situation is similar to that in 1683, when the Turks were outside Vienna. At that time military reinforcements came over the Kahlenberg; today—nothing like that is to be expected. . . . If our city falls, then the Prussian barbarians will swamp Europe." This time Freud ended with a dream of travel and change—and of hope: "I should like to live in England . . . ," Freud said, "and travel to Rome, like you."

The Nazi troops who entered Austria that Saturday morning enjoyed a glorious welcome. Crowds swarmed the streets to greet them, throwing flowers in their path. Troops eventually received orders to keep their goggles down lest the flowers harm their eyes. All through Austria members of the once-banned Nazi Party began turning their swastika lapel buttons outward and exchanging the salute with each other on the street. Hitler himself flew to Munich and from there began driving to the Austrian border in an open-topped Mercedes, accompanied by a bodyguard of SS troops. At ten minutes of four in the afternoon—close to the time Freud was reading the newspaper headlines and throwing the paper across the room—Adolf Hitler arrived at his birthplace, Braunau am Inn, where screaming crowds met him.

Four hours later, Hitler was in the city of Linz. Church bells rang and a mob gathered in front of the town hall, and began the chant: "One People! One Nation! One Leader! / One People! One Nation! One Leader!"

"Any further attempt to tear the people apart," Hitler cried from the balcony of the town hall, "will be in vain." The führer laid flowers on the graves of his parents and, after visiting his old home, went back to his hotel to dream the future.

The reception he got in Linz shocked Hitler. He had hoped that the Austrians would acquiesce to the German takeover. He planned to form a confederacy with Austria, in which Germany would be the dominant partner. But far from being merely compliant, the Austrians who greeted Hitler along the road and who gathered beneath his balcony in Linz were in ecstasy. They saluted the führer as if he were their savior: they knew that Hitler would deliver them from their poverty and their weakness and from the chief source of all their troubles, the Jews. That night in the hotel, Hitler saw that he could hope for more than a confederacy: he could annex the entire nation and do what he liked with its resources and its inhabitants. He could make Austria what he would eventually want every sovereign state in the world to be, a dependent province of Germany. His ambitions burning, Hitler set out for Vienna, Sigmund Freud, and a hundred and seventy thousand other Jewish men and women and children.

"Vienna was scarcely recognizable this morning," wrote Shirer of that Saturday. "Swastika flags [were] flying from nearly every house. Where did they get them so fast?"

Finis Austria, the End of Austria—the words Freud wrote in his journal that Saturday meant something specific and painful to their author. They meant the end of a culture, centered in Vienna, that was cosmopolitan, at least ostensibly tolerant, not lacking in sophistication, devoted to art and science—and relatively safe for the Jews. During Freud's boyhood several

Jews had actually served in the Austro-Hungarian ministry. Looking back, Freud said that, at the time, Jewish schoolboys went around with ministers' portfolios stashed in their schoolbags—a sign of their possible destinies—much as common soldiers in Napoleon's army had gone off to war carrying field marshal's batons. Freud's life had unfolded in a city that some people have described as Wittgenstein's Vienna. It was a city that, from the end of the First World War and the dissolution of the Austro-Hungarian Empire until March of 1938—until the moment, one might say, when Sigmund Freud threw his newspaper across the room—had been a center of art and learning. This was the Vienna of Karl Kraus, perhaps the most brilliant satirist of the modern period. It was the Vienna of Robert Musil, author of the modernist masterwork *The Man Without Qualities*. Here Arnold Schoenberg made his breakthroughs in twelve-tone musical composition. In Vienna, Adolf Loos developed his version of a modernist architecture. And in Vienna, perhaps most consequentially, Ludwig Wittgenstein offered a new start for philosophy, attempting to sweep away virtually all prior work in the field, and getting back to basic problems and basic propositions.

Vienna hummed with new and consequential happenings everywhere, of innovations issuing from the artists and intellectuals directed toward an alert, intelligent public. No doubt the atmosphere was at times an inspiration to Freud. But while many—and perhaps even the most gifted and original—of his contemporaries were seeking clarity, elegance, and mathematical precision, in perfect aphorisms, geometrically precise architectural designs, and pared-down philosophical treatises, which passed over all things that could not be rigorously said in silence, Freud moved in a different direction. His work was a dramatic contrast to the international, Apollonian style that characterized a significant quotient of the Viennese revolution in culture.

Freud's thinking moved backward into the dark past—rather than forward into the highly reasoned future. "He would have us remember most of all," as Auden put it in his beautiful elegy for Freud, "to be enthusiastic over the night." Freud was absorbed by what was old, atavistic, uncanny, and heretofore undecipherable. He was fascinated by things that most of Vienna's elite artists and thinkers would have considered ridiculous. (Wittgenstein, probably the most gifted and original of the group—and rightly renowned for his intellectual honesty—found Freud's work to be both alluring and misleading: he called it "a very powerful mythology.") After his book on dreams, Freud wrote one about slips of the tongue and the pen; soon afterward came a full-length book about jokes. He brooded on childhood eros in his notorious *Essays on the Theory of Sexuality*. Childhood, folktales, dreams, eccentric day-to-day behavior, the unwell, the marginal and the misunderstood—Freud was intrigued by the kinds of people and things that grandmothers sitting around the hearth gossiped over.

To Freud, the only way to move forward as a civilization was to face the repressed—the disordered accumulation that was packed down in the cellars and crypts of the psyche. It would be hard to argue that any of Freud's prominent contemporaries in art and intellectual life, with the possible exception of the satirist Karl Kraus, were doing work that could have prepared Vienna and the world for what would happen in March of 1938. There is nothing to be found in the *Tractatus* of Wittgenstein—who actually went to school with Hitler for a while and may be referred to in a passage in *Mein Kampf* about an aloof Jewish boy—that looks ahead to the horror of the 1930s.

To many middle-class Viennese, Wittgenstein's Vienna (which was in some measure Freud's Vienna too) was an exhilarating place. They took themselves to be at the heart of the intellectual and artistic world. But Vienna in the 1930s became socially and politically an extremely turbulent place. The depression of 1929 hit Austria particularly hard: in May of 1931, Vienna's largest commercial bank, the Creditanstalt, declared itself insolvent; by February of 1933, a quarter of the labor force was unemployed. A year later, came the February uprising, in which the Social Democrats and Bolsheviks of what was called Red Vienna rebelled, only to be murderously put down by the government of Engelbert Dollfuss. Less than six months later, in July of 1934, came the attempted coup, in which Dollfuss himself was killed by the Nazis and Hitler nearly invaded.

Though Freud's financial situation was relatively secure in the early and mid-1930s—he had foreign patients who paid him well—many of the people around him in Vienna were suffering. "The human cost [of the depression] was incalculable," Peter Gay observes. "Personal tragedies—promising careers aborted, sudden poverty, educated men selling shoelaces or apples on street corners, proud bourgeois taking handouts from their relatives—became commonplace everywhere."

The Viennese were encountering a version of the world that Karl Marx was expert at describing: this is the world of capitalism amok, in which the preeminent values are monetary values. In this world there are no stabilities, because nothing that cannot produce profits, or somehow lend itself to profit production, will stay intact for long. As Marx put it, in lines that for many would have characterized Vienna from the end of the First World War until the day that Hitler and his troops crossed the border: "Constant revolutionizing of production, uninterrupted disturbance of all social conditions, everlasting uncertainty and agitation distinguish the bourgeois epoch from all earlier ones. All fixed, fast-frozen relations, with their train of ancient and venerable prejudices and opinions are swept away, all new-formed ones become antiquated before they can ossify. All that is solid melts into air, all that is holy is profaned."

Freud was both old and new. What he said about the psyche was shockingly novel and, as such, a part of the Viennese cultural revolution. Yet what he said also drew on old wisdom; Freud compounded his work not only from clinical observation, but from reading Sophocles, Shakespeare, and Milton. He also drew on fairy tales and folk wisdom, as well as that fund of information—to him often closer to the truth than the educated believe—everyday common sense.

Freud's response to the crisis of the age was complex: look backward in order to look to the future, he seemed to say. Hitler and the Nazis had a way of dealing with the world where "all that is solid melts into air" too. Their way was to bring the present under control through the triumph of one leader, one party, one race, and one nation. They insisted on oneness in a world that seemed to be flying apart into unmanageable fragments. The Austrians who, on those March days, began turning their swastika lapel buttons out for the world and their Jewish neighbors to see, were hoping for many things, but one of them was deliverance from the world that Marx had so aptly described into a world of comforting, if brutal, simplifications. Hitler, who, on Monday, March 14, was heading to Vienna (and to Freud), seemed to many the man best able to solve the problems of modernity.

For his part, Freud began to make preparations. The night before the führer's arrival in the city, Freud called a meeting of the Vienna Psychoanalytical Society at Berggasse 19. There he shook hands individually with each of the members, saying, quite simply, "There is nothing one can do about it." The decision was to disband the society, with the possibility of reforming it wherever Freud might settle, assuming he could— or wanted to—find a way out of Vienna at all.

The Nazis had not, as one might have expected, closed the Berlin Psychoanalytical Institute when they gained power in 1933. Rather, they had taken it over, begun discharging the Jewish analysts, and put it under the direction of one M. H. Göring, a cousin of Hermann Göring, Hitler's eventual Reichsmarschall. The Nazis associated with psychoanalysis generally thought that Freud was right, almost word for word. All he had written was valid: psychoanalysis was in fact a science. However, they added one qualification. Psychoanalysis was a Jewish science, which meant not only that a Jew had created it and other Jews had developed it, but that by and large its findings applied to Jews and to Jews only. Jews, it seems, were people beset by the Oedipal complex; possessing—and possessed by—a violent, sexually charged unconscious; prone to infantile sexuality. All that Freud said was so—but it was so about the Jews. Not long after the Nazi takeover, Carl Jung gave a sequence of lectures at the new institute in Berlin in which he made some theoretical observations about the singularity of the Aryan psyche and its contrast to what he thought of as the psyche of the Jews. "The Aryan unconscious," Jung observed, "has a higher potential than the Jewish; that is the advantage and the disadvantage of a youthfulness not yet fully estranged from barbarism." The theoretical work of the Göring Institute was to compound a comprehensive theory of Aryan psychology, given that a Jewish psychology was already so well in place.

On the afternoon of March 14, Adolf Hitler returned to the great city of his youth. He rode through the streets of Vienna in the open-topped Mercedes, standing up, holding on to the car's windshield with his left hand, with his right returning the salute to the crowds massed to greet him. Almost every prominent building was draped with the German flag. There were swastikas everywhere and the crowds were screaming. Yet Hitler was distracted. He gave little indication that he even took the people in. His salute appeared to be halfhearted, perfunctory; he seemed to be hardly holding on to the windshield. What's striking is how vulnerable the führer allowed himself to be. He was completely exposed to the crowd and at the mercy of any halfway able assassin. Yet he proceeded with an absolute, if somnambular, confidence; he was sure, it seems, that no one in Vienna could mean him serious harm.

Hitler's car stopped in front of the Imperial Hotel, a place that he had often dreamed of entering when he was living at the men's shelter. Now it was decked with a huge red banner emblazoned with the swastika. Even after Hitler entered the hotel and made his way to the royal suite, the crowd stayed outside, chanting a variation on an old German drinking song: "We won't go home, we won't go home," they cried, "until the führer speaks!" The mob sang on into the night, and Hitler showed himself again and again from the hotel.

As the evening passed, Hitler began reminiscing about the feelings he had for the Imperial Hotel when he lived in Vienna thirty years ago. He fell into one of his amazing bouts of speech: Hitler, as a Don DeLillo character says, "called himself the lonely wanderer out of nothingness. He sucked on lozenges, spoke to people in endless monologues, free associating, as if the language came from some vastness beyond the world and he was simply the medium of revelation." And so the führer seems to have spoken that night.

"I could see the glittering lights and chandeliers in the lobby," Hitler said to his companions in the suite, "but I knew it was impossible for me to set foot inside. One night, after a bad blizzard which piled up several feet of snow, I had a chance to make some money for food by shoveling snow. Ironically enough, the five or six of us in my group were sent to clean the street and sidewalk in front of the Imperial Hotel." Members of the royal family, the Hapsburgs, were at the hotel that night, and Hitler remembered them well. "I saw Karl and Zita step out of their imperial coach and grandly walk into this hotel over the red carpet. We poor devils shoveled the snow away on all sides and took our hats off every time the aristocrats arrived. They didn't even look at us, although I still smell the perfume that came to our noses. We were about as important to them, or for that matter to Vienna, as the snow that kept coming down all night, and this hotel did not even have the decency to send out a cup of hot coffee to us." The music that Hitler heard coming from inside was so beautiful that it made him want to weep, but it also made him rage about the injustice of what was happening to him. "I resolved that night," Hitler said, "that some day I would come back to the Imperial Hotel and walk over the red carpet in that glittering interior where the Hapsburgs danced. I didn't know how or when, but I have waited for this day and tonight I am here."

The next day, Tuesday, March 15, which would be a sadly memorable one for Sigmund Freud, Hitler woke up without the stomach cramps that had bothered him in Linz. The führer had a tender digestive system and unaccustomed food could play havoc with it. In the afternoon, a quarter of a million Viennese gathered in the Heldenplatz, the Hero's Square, and Hitler exuberantly announced that Austria was now part of the German Reich; the nation had a new name, Ostmark. "A Legitimist leader," Hitler declared, "once described the task of Austria's so-called independence as that of hindering the construction of a really great German Reich. I now proclaim for this land a new mission. The oldest eastern province of the German people shall from now on be the youngest bulwark of the German nation."

Finally, in front of the 250,000, he congratulated himself: "I can in this hour report before history the conclusion of the greatest aim in my life: the entry of my homeland into the German Reich."

As soon as the German troops crossed the border into Austria, Jews in Vienna began coming under attack. All through the streets, Jews were being stopped by gangs of storm troopers who kicked, punched, and humiliated them. Nazis broke into Jewish homes and businesses, beat up everyone on the premises, and took what they wanted. The streets became a sort of black carnival, an urban hell, where all the bottled-up racial hatred of the last decades exploded into the open. Shirer, the American journalist, saw Jews on their hands and knees scrubbing nationalist slogans off the sidewalk as jeering storm troopers stood over them and crowds taunted. "Many Jews killing themselves," Shirer observed. Hundreds of Jewish men and women were taken into custody to clean latrines for the Nazis, sometimes with implements, sometimes with their hands. The storm troopers rounded up elderly white bearded Jews, brought them to the synagogues and compelled them to do deep knee bends, while they chanted "Heil Hitler."

Franz Danimann, who lived in Schwechat, a suburb of Vienna, recalled what happened to the Jewish businesspeople in his district. They were driven onto the street by Nazis, given toothbrushes, and told to get down on their knees and clean. Finally, the Nazis said, the Jews would learn how to work. "They were heartbreaking scenes," Danimann recalled. "The victims were often old people, but despite the fact that they were forced to kneel down to the work, they managed to retain their dignity."

Danimann, who was a Social Democrat and not a Jew, accosted one of the storm troopers, asking if he wasn't ashamed of his behavior. The Nazi replied, "Ah, so you are a friend of theirs, are you? Well for you we can find another toothbrush. Get down on your knees and start scrubbing." Danimann jumped onto his bicycle and rode away. Not much later, he was arrested; ultimately he went to Auschwitz.

Shirer's wife, Tess, was in the hospital to deliver a baby. A Jewish woman she met there was grieving for her brother-in-law, who had committed suicide the day Hitler entered Vienna. She left the hospital in black mourning dress, holding on to her newborn child. Another woman, about to give birth, learned that the Nazis had taken away her husband's business and looted their apartment. "She fears her husband will be killed or arrested," Tess told Shirer, "and weeps all night long."

A few days earlier, Shirer and his fellow correspondent Edward R. Murrow had gone out late for a drink. They stopped into a bar and sat down, but Murrow was obviously uncomfortable. He told Shirer that they had to leave. Why? Shirer liked it there and wanted to stay. Finally Murrow explained. Last night, he had been at the same place and "a Jewish looking fellow" standing at the bar took an old-fashioned straight razor out of his pocket and slashed his throat with it.

Jews were trying to leave the city, but almost as soon as the German troops crossed the border, young Austrian storm troopers dispatched themselves to the train stations and intercepted most of them. The Jews who tried to escape were sent back to Vienna and often put under arrest. Then the Nazis made for their homes and began stealing what they could. In all, the Nazis arrested 21,000 people during the first days of the Anschluss and sent them off to Dachau. By the end of the year, all but 1,500 had been released, though many who went free then would be captured again and sent to the concentration camps.

From those early days of the annexation, certain photographic images stand out. One is a picture of a large man, his belly pressed tight against his fully buttoned jacket. He wears lace-up boots, knee socks with knickers, and a soft hat. He looks to be a man who enjoys mountain climbing, beer, and his breakfast. On his face is an expression of surpassing distaste, as though he takes himself to be an important executive of some sort, overseeing a highly consequential but rather repulsive project. Behind the man and to his right, a crowd of eight or so people is gathered, looking on with approval. A young boy about ten years old kneels in front of the man, facing the wall of a building. The boy's flexible posture, one knee bent almost gracefully outward, is in marked contrast to the man's stiff, stolid presence. The boy has a can of paint in his left hand and with his right he wields a brush. A rectangular block protrudes slightly from the face of the building, and on that block, the boy is painting the word *Jude*, Jew. He is painting the front of his father's business, at the insistence of the stolid man, so that the people will know it is a Jewish business and avoid it.

Another image. A Viennese crowd is in the street and scuffling with police. The police have linked their hands to form a human rope. They are holding on tight, but the mass of people is pushing hard against them, making it difficult to maintain order. The police are well turned out in jackboots and neat military caps. One of them, probably an officer, directs them as effectively as he can, but their case may be hopeless. Behind the human lines there are some men, but most who have made it to the front are women. Some of the women are smiling, some laughing, some seem nearly ecstatic. Clearly, the police are only pretending to disapprove of the crowd's passion; really they are enjoying it, playing the role of authorities, when in fact they're as happy and excited as the crowd. Behind them is a Nazi flag, about twenty feet high, hanging on a lamppost. The people are waiting for Hitler to come and address them and they are showing all the vitality and mock rebelliousness that girls and boys at rock concerts, about thirty years and a world away, will show.

The Nazis threw Jews in prison; they confiscated businesses that had taken generations to build; they invaded apartment buildings, tossed the residents out on the street, and moved in themselves. They insulted and spit on mothers and fathers in front of their children. But they also visited smaller indignities on the Jews, banning them from certain park benches, restricting their movements. Matters of dirt and contamination obsessed the Nazis. They wanted the Jews to be cleaning things, streets and latrines. They wanted to limit the contact between Jews and gentiles, lest the Jews pass them some sort of infection. This obsession with cleanliness and hygiene, this concern with purity, which took off so violently in Austria, would eventually come to dominate the Nazis. In time, Jews were not to clean, or sanitize on their own, but to be cleaned away.

Many who observed the events in Austria after the Anschluss were shocked by them. They could not imagine that anyone, not even the Nazis, could act so brutally. The Germans, it seemed, had embraced anti-Semitism much more slowly. It had taken five years, the years since Hitler came to power, for the Germans to commit themselves fully to race hatred. Even now, in March of 1938, it was probably safer to be a Jew in Berlin than to be one in Vienna. (One observer declared that the Germans were excellent Nazis but rather poor anti-Semites; but that the Austrians, though inept enough as Nazis, were highly accomplished in their anti-Semitism.) The Viennese, purportedly among the most tolerant people in all of Europe, rose to rabid violence against the Jews in just a few days. Stefan Zweig, a friend of Freud's, and himself a Jew, was horrified by the events of March: "All the sickly, unclean fantasies of hate that had been conceived in many orgiastic nights found raging expression in bright daylight."

Zweig's shock is not difficult to understand. Vienna's more refined residents were not only proud of their city's culture, they also took Vienna to be a center of enlightened social tolerance. The city was multiracial and multinational: here one found not only Germans, but Czechs, Slovaks, Poles, Ruthenians, Slovenians, Serbo-Croats, Magyars, Romanians, and Italians. Certainly there were a number of anti-Semitic publications, which carried stories and cartoons depicting Jews in ways that were, to say the least, distasteful. From 1897 to 1910, Vienna had an anti-

Semitic mayor, Karl Lueger, whom Hitler greatly admired, calling him "the mightiest mayor of all time." (Freud detested Lueger, once celebrating one of his political reversals with a forbidden cigar.) Still most liberal observers thought of pre-Anschluss Vienna as a relative paradise for European Jews.

Anyone who had been reading Freud though would not have been terribly surprised at the events of March 1938. Ever attentive to the sadistic side of humanity, Freud believed that even the most apparently civilized people nurse fantasies of violence, rape, and plunder. To Freud, we are all in our hearts criminals. "Our dreams convince us that these things are so," he said, in one form or another, time after time. The forces that divide us from our most disturbing desires—the ego, reason, civilization—are potent, to be sure. But their potency is diminished when unconscious desires are inflamed by external events. Freud believed that what we dream at night we can, given certain circumstances, enact in waking life. In his reflections on the Anschluss, Freud shows irritation, impatience, and occasionally something approaching a dark bemusement, but he is never shocked. He had been studying the unconscious for too long.

Nor does Hitler seem to surprise him much. It is strange but true: Freud is always scandalized by the thought of America, but he often seems to take Hitler and the Nazis as simple facts of life. Perhaps that is because for twenty-five years, authority, and particularly the sort of authority that Hitler embodied, had been at the center of Freud's concerns as a writer and thinker, and also of his practice as a therapist. Reflecting on the Nazis, well after the takeover of Austria, Freud told Arthur Koestler that they were merely expressing a commonplace sort of human aggression. "Something like this was inevitable," Freud said. "I am not sure that from my standpoint I can blame them."

Up until 1914, Freud had been transfixed by the workings of the unconscious. He was absorbed in his studies of dreams and folktales, slips of the tongue and the pen, jokes, children, fantasies, and art. He was absorbed, too, in his case studies. He told the stories of the Wolf Man and the Rat Man, Dora and Emma, and all the rest. Freud was always a relatively dark writer, but one can find a certain measured optimism in his developing view that in the simple, often-forgotten corners of human life, there is meaning to be found—and that in such meaning there lies hope for freedom from psychological misery. By becoming more conversant with their desires, Freud suggested time and again, human beings might expect a little less renunciation from themselves and so might become a little freer, more at peace. We need not act out every repressed desire—Freud was too much a realist to believe that we should. But simply by attaching words to out deepest wishes, making conscious what had been repressed, we might achieve a level of self-acceptance that would lead to some tranquility and—who knows?—maybe a glint of happiness from time to time. Where "it" was, Freud said, there "I" shall be, and in saying as much he gestured toward an intellectual and spiritual path that would lead not to salvation, to be sure, but to a better life. This was the Freud who, as Peter Gay acutely observed, taught the world that there was more to understand and less to judge about people than most had previously imagined.

But beginning in about 1914, traces of optimism become less

and less common in Freud's work. For he had, he thought, hit upon a fundamental difficulty in human life: the problem of authority. Human beings, Freud came to believe, are addicted to authority and often to destructive authority at that. Frequently our strongest desire, oddly enough, is to find a figure who will control our desires. We wish to be dominated. We wish to submit.

Freud saw this hunger for domination manifest in many areas of experience, but nowhere so potently, or so dangerously, as in politics. In 1921, when Hitler's political career was just beginning, Freud published *Group Psychology and the Analysis of the Ego*, a study of crowd behavior that lays special emphasis on the role of the leader. The world, in this vision, is a disturbing, complex, sometimes chaotic place where everything that has been solid and sound melts into the air. Values, if they exist at all, are in flux. But then comes the leader, who appears to be certain about all things. "His intellectual acts," Freud wrote, are "strong and independent even in isolation, and his will need[s] no reinforcement from others." Where others are buffeted by doubts, the leader is always sure that his vision is the one true vision. His ego has few emotional ties; he loves no one but himself and to others he gives away no more than the bare minimum of affection or recognition. "Members of a group," Freud continued, "stand in need of the illusion that they are equally and justly loved by their leader; but the leader himself need love no one else, he may be of a masterful nature, absolutely narcissistic, self-confident and independent. We know that love puts a check on narcissism"—and the leader is the ultimate figure of self-enclosed self-love. In his insistence on the centrality of the leader and the dynamics of his relation to the group, Freud pressed beyond the work of predecessors like Gustav Le Bon, who, to Freud's way of thinking, overemphasized the power of the collective mind in and of itself. Le Bon believed that when a group forms, a special consciousness rises up, one that is markedly different from individual consciousness, but not determined by the presence of the leader. To Freud, crowds on their own can be dangerous—he was as wary of them as two of his favorite authors, Charles Dickens and Mark Twain, were—but he suggested that crowds only constitute a long-term murderous threat when a certain sort of figure takes over the leader role in ways that are both prohibitive and permissive.

The description that Freud offers of the leader eerily anticipates the kinds of descriptions that Hitler's followers began to offer about him, starting in the 1920s. Here, finally, was a politician with an uncompromising way of seeing the world and a clear program. He knew what he hated: Jews, the Versailles Treaty (he called it "the stab in the back"), Marxists. He knew what he wanted: the unification of the German people, a strong army, complete dedication to the state, an empire. He said that for Germany to come into its own, the people would have to look to a great leader and find in him the sublime expression of their will. He was that leader. Providence had appointed him. Such a leader did not need to consult the people or their representatives from moment to moment. No, his relation to them was nearly mystical, for he embodied their will. He embodied all of their highest aspirations, *whether they were aware of those aspirations or not.* Hitler was never in doubt. He always knew the Truth and proclaimed it with absolute conviction.

In another sense, of course, Hitler was an absurd figure. The man who so fiercely endorsed the Aryan ideal was himself short, dark, and homely, with a ridiculous mustache. He spoke in mangled sentences; his writing was full of misspellings and puerile grammatical errors. His idea of the good life consisted of sitting around a lunch table with a collection of lackeys, eating sweet pastries and holding forth on his two favorite subjects, his war experiences and the loyalty of dogs. In the evening he watched operettas on film, then, when they were over, went back to talking about his war experiences and praising the loyalty of dogs. In private he could be astonishingly emotional—he was prone to weep—and out of focus. But when he needed to, Hitler was highly accomplished at playing the role that Freud describes, the role of the masterful man who knows the truth and is untroubled by doubts. (Hitler's biographer, John Toland, speculates that Hitler may have read *Group Psychology* and used it to guide his performances. Yet there is no hard evidence for this; nor is there evidence for Hitler having read any intellectually demanding book and taken in its meaning. He claimed to adore Schopenhauer, but he misunderstood *The World as Will and Representation* almost entirely.) Hitler was especially appealing to young people and to women; when they heard him, they seemed to feel, as Goebbels, the most devoted of Hitler's sycophants, observed, that a new messiah had come at last into the world.

* * *

On the day that Hitler addressed the citizens of Vienna, announcing to them and to the world that he had absorbed Austria into the Reich, a gang of Nazis invaded the Verlag, the printing press that published Freud's books. The press was at Berggasse 7, just a few doors away from Freud's apartment, and Freud's son Martin, a lawyer, was there already, doing what he could to dispose of the records, when the Nazis arrived. Papers stored at the Verlag revealed that Freud, like many Viennese Jews, had placed money in foreign accounts. This was now illegal. If the Nazis discovered it, they would surely confiscate the funds, and perhaps jail Freud and his family too.

Martin had not been at the Verlag long when the gang broke in. There were about a dozen of them, Martin recalled, shabbily dressed, not in uniform, but well armed. Almost all carried rifles, except for one small, worn-out-looking man, who came in with a drawn pistol. When Martin seemed uncooperative, the small man pushed the pistol into his belly and said, "Why not shoot him now and be finished with him? We should shoot him on the spot." Quickly the Nazis got into the safe, emptied its contents on the desk, and began combing through them.

The situation was dangerous, but also rather grotesque. The men facing Martin Freud that day were not, it appears, hard-core Nazi ideologues. Rather they were anti-Semitic thugs looking to get what profit they could in the confusion that reigned everywhere in Vienna. It was open season on Jews and Jewish property and they were not going to be left out. The encounter with Martin vacillated from raw threat, with the disheveled man poking his victim with the pistol, to something bordering on dark comedy. At a certain point, Martin petitioned the group for a cup of tea. This was put to a vote, and it was decided that yes, it would be all right, provided that Martin wash his own cup and saucer. Martin requested that the office boy wash them, and this too was put to a vote and approved, even though the office boy had converted to Nazism at about the moment the gang arrived.

Suddenly Ernest Jones, Freud's devoted disciple, appeared in the office. Jones had flown in from London as soon as he heard about the Anschluss and had rushed to the press to see what he could do. Nothing, it turned out: the men wouldn't listen to him and so he went off to find what Martin Freud rather optimistically called "a more responsible Nazi authority."

In the early afternoon, Martin was left alone with one of the Nazis, a melancholy-looking, middle-aged man, who seemed more like a headwaiter than a soldier. The guard told him a tale about the hardships and privations he had endured in recent years and soon it became clear to Martin that what he most wanted was money. Martin gave him all he had in his pockets, some gold coins and a roll of notes. The guard was so grateful that he began honoring Martin's multiple requests to use the bathroom. Time after time, Martin went down the corridor, on each visit scooping up a handful of compromising documents and flushing them away.

It turned out that across the street from the Verlag lived a Nazi who was watching the proceedings through his window. He saw that when Martin and his guard left the room, other members of the gang crept back in and pocketed the coins and bills that were lying on the table. A disgrace to the party, this was inexcusable. The outraged Nazi called party head-quarters and in time the district commander of the SA made his way to the press, huffing and puffing. Apparently he had run all the way. "Young and erect of stature," Martin recalled, "he radiated an authority which had an immediate effect on the rabble that had been tormenting me for so long. They fell in at his sharp command and after one or two had been ordered to remain to clear up the mess in the office, the main body marched off." Left standing in the corner was the original guard, the headwaiter manqué, who had been frisked and found with Martin's money in his pocket.

While the Nazis were breaking up, Anna Freud arrived and received all the courtesy of the Reich. The commander gave Anna and Martin a pass they could use to make their way to Nazi headquarters the next day without being stopped and harassed on the street. The last thing the commander did was to dismiss the melancholy waiter, giving him back his rifle, but not the coins and currency that Martin had passed his way.

There is a semi-farcical quality to the events of that after-noon, or at least to Martin's account of them. But what seemed absurd could quickly have become dangerous, maybe deadly. All over Vienna similar gangs, armed and decked with swastikas, were making the rounds. Often all they did was steal. But some Jews were badly beaten, some Jews murdered. And of course all this was only a prelude to deeper horrors.

Freud was surely disturbed to learn of the threat to Martin that day, but the thought of his daughter Anna being on the scene and in danger would have been almost more than he could bear.

Freud's love for Anna was by now nearly beyond description. She was his Cordelia and, as he often said, his Antigone as well. Anna was the great comfort of his old age and also his hope for the future. What Freud wanted was not to live on and on; he was tired and sick now and at times seemed ready to leave the world. What he wanted was to depart life convinced that the movement he founded would live on through time. Freud was obsessed with the continuity of his work and lately he had come to see that Anna might be the one who could do the most to achieve it.

He had not always held his youngest child in such esteem. Anna was not pretty and she was not precocious; as a girl, she was dutiful, thoughtful, and thorough, with a capacity for work that wasn't unlike Freud's. Over time, though, Freud came to see that what Anna lacked in quickness of understanding, she made up for in depth. She immersed herself in his work and in his world—when she was still a girl, she sat in on the seminars Freud held for his disciples at Berggasse 19 in a room blue with cigar smoke—and became as well versed in his thought as any of his followers. Her relation to Freud's vision was never what could be called creative. She took it all in; she learned its terms by heart; but it never seems to have occurred to Anna that her father's thinking required anything by way of revision or even much development.

Freud's authority with Anna was absolute and he had established it early in her life in part by psychoanalyzing her himself. Looking back on the psychoanalysis, Anna said that her father never permitted her to indulge in half measures. He compelled her to offer the whole truth about everything, including her erotic life. She shared with him her sexual fantasies and her forays into masturbation, and Freud took it all in with his characteristic equanimity. Anna emerged from the analysis grateful to her father and more committed to him than ever. From that time on, Freud's attitude toward his daughter was protective in the extreme, especially when sex was the issue. Even as Anna reached her twenties and began to attract men, including the devoted womanizer Ernest Jones, Freud continually proclaimed that she was too young and not at all ready to leave the family. Once, during the period of Anna's analysis, when she had gone off on vacation and left her mother and father, Freud wrote to Lou Andreas-Salomé, saying that "I have long felt sorry for her for still being at home with us old folks . . . but on the other hand, if she really were to go away, I should feel myself as deprived as I do now, and as I should do if I had to give up smoking!"

Anna Freud's closest relationship aside from the one with her father was with Dorothy Burlingham, an American woman who arrived in Vienna in 1925, where she was analyzed by Theodor Reik and then by Freud. She also had her four children analyzed and was so impressed by the results that she herself trained to be a child analyst. Dorothy Burlingham became attached to the Freud family and particularly to Anna: the two of them traveled together in Italy in 1927. Yet as close as Dorothy came to Anna, as constant as was their companionship, it is almost certain that there was no overtly sexual relation between the two. Anna was and remained her father's.

By 1938, Anna had virtually displaced her mother, Martha, in Freud's life. Anna took care of Freud, she got his medicine, she helped him remove and clean the prosthesis on the right side of his jaw, she made sure that he was comfortable. And, also, Anna sustained him intellectually, for he talked his ideas over with her as much as he did with anyone. He sought her comfort, yes, but he also sought her intellectual advice. Anna had become Freud's great stay against the world. In a letter to Ernst, Freud's architect son who was living in London, two months before the Anschluss, Freud said, "Anna is splendid in spirits, achievement, and in all human relationships. It is amazing how clear and independent her scientific work has become. If she had more ambition . . . but perhaps it is better like this for her later life."

Freud loved his daughter for all she was and all she brought to him day after day, but there was also a pragmatic dimension to his attachment. Part of Freud's genius lay in knowing that to be a genius was not enough. Freud had a comprehensive and brilliant vision about what life was and, implicitly, of how it might be lived. Good: so had others. The pressing task now, in 1938, was to make certain that the vision would survive over time. Freud could look back into recent German intellectual history and see two thinkers, Schopenhauer and Nietzsche, whose achievements were comparable to his own—perhaps they were even more original. But would their work live on? Both had left academia early in life. Neither had founded a school;

neither had created disciples in significant numbers or set up an institutional structure to ensure that their ideas would outlive them and circulate throughout the world. Freud did not want to make such a mistake.

For at least the past thirty years, Freud had sought inheritors, younger men (it would preferably be men) who could devote themselves to him and continue his legacy. He gathered around him talented figures like Karl Abraham, Sándor Ferenczi, and Carl Jung. He seated them at the table, with himself at the head, like a monarch surrounded by his knights. In time, he gave some of them rings, to seal the fellowship. He called them his sons. (His actual sons were, Freud had to admit, solid and sensible young men, but without the kind of intellectual talent that he most valued.) Freud, in other words, behaved something like the primal father he described in *Totem and Taboo* and also not entirely unlike the leader he described in *Group Psychology*, the man with the masterly aura. He lorded it over a horde of surrogate sons. And then, what he said in *Totem and Taboo* about the dynamics of tribal authority proved to be true, or nearly true, even in the purportedly civilized world of Vienna.

In *Totem and Taboo*, the climax of the tribal story comes when the sons rise up, kill the father, and eat him. (They believe him to be magic and want to internalize his supernatural powers.) Their guilt at what they have done causes them to idealize his image and to worship him in the time to come. Thus is religion founded. The book comes close to describing—in melodramatic enough terms—the dynamics of Freud's own urge to achieve authority. Freud managed to mesmerize his adoptive sons, not only with his originality and brilliance, but also with his frequent willingness to play the role of the patriarch. The sons, eventually, revolted—or at least the most talented of them usually did. Jung, the "crown prince," was the most promising of the inheritors and also the most rebellious, for Jung demanded to think for himself. He disagreed with Freud on many things, perhaps most significantly about his vision of the unconscious. To Jung, the unconscious was not the seat of repressed and dangerous desires. Rather, the unconscious was a repository of collective wisdom. Here one found figures—wise men and women, wizards, tricksters, the cast of the world's mythology—who offered wisdom to the individual locked in a repressive existence.

That Jung, who had learned all he knew from Freud, was ready to announce, in his gypsy way, that the unconscious was more sane and creative than the conscious mind—to Freud, this was too much to bear. Look outside in the street now, look into Vienna, where the unconscious, unmediated by any sane authority, is having its day, and see what you think, Freud might have reflected during those March weeks, for his thoughts, even many years after the break, were often full of Jung.

Over time, in fact, Freud could not bear much of any intellectual disagreement from his followers. The story goes that when a disciple once disputed a point with him during a seminar, Freud tried to quash him. "But," the disciple replied, "a dwarf sitting on the shoulders of a giant can see farther than the giant." Freud took this in. He gestured with his cigar once, then again. "Fine," the founder replied, "but a louse sitting on the head of an astronomer, what can he see?"

Carl Jung was creative; he was a visionary and a mystic and he impressed Freud and disturbed him in about equal measure. To break with Jung, as Freud did beginning around 1912, and to choose Anna as the guardian of the legacy was a great shift. In making it, Freud chose caution over imagination, continuity over creative disjunction. That Anna's best-known book is *The Ego and the Mechanisms of Defense* is entirely apt, for Anna was becoming a defense mechanism, not only for the ego that was Freud, but for his entire legacy. In time, she would set out to turn her father's work, which was sometimes nearly as speculative and wild as anything Jung ever wrote, into a coherent, stable, and sensible doctrine.

Freud loved Anna for herself; he passionately wanted her happiness—that much is certain. But he also loved her as a guarantor of the only kind of immortality that Freud, the self-professed godless Jew, could believe in.

Soon another group of Nazis—some of them perhaps from the gang that had invaded the Verlag—appeared at the door of Berggasse 19, where they were met by Martha Freud. Martha looked them over, stood aside, and let the Nazis into the apartment. Ever the good Viennese housewife, she asked the men as they entered if they might care to leave their rifles in the umbrella stand set by the door. This courtesy they declined.

When the Nazis arrived on that March day, Freud was sequestered at the back of Berggasse 19, in his private domain. To regather his strength, Freud had taken to lying on his famous couch atop a thick, richly woven oriental rug, propped up with a half dozen or so pillows. There was a second carpet fastened to the wall behind the couch, giving Freud, the convalescent, what it gave his patients, a sense of enclosure and warmth. At the foot of the couch where Freud lay, a small stove burned to fend off Vienna's winter chill. Close by the stove sat Freud's beloved dog, his chow, Lün, snoring and panting and filling the air with her rich canine scent.

Here Freud was surrounded by his massive collection of antiquities and by tributes to great civilizations past. Over Freud's head hung a large colored rendering of the Egyptian cliff temple of Ramses II at Abu Simbel. At the head of his couch, directly behind him in the corner, was a bust of an earnest Roman citizen, and above the bust, Pompeiian-style wall paintings of a centaur and of the great god Pan. At the couch's foot, close by the stove, were a number of pictures, including a reproduction of the famous painting by Ingres that depicts Oedipus interrogating the sphinx. When Freud celebrated his fiftieth birthday, his disciples gave him a medallion that showed Freud himself conducting an exchange with the creature.

When Freud turned right from where he lay on the couch, he saw a bookcase full of his antiquities, small statues, busts, and vases from ancient Egypt, Greece, and Rome, as well as a few from China and India. Freud had over two thousand such pieces and they were posed everywhere, including on the floor, in his section of the house.

On the bookcase was a large Chinese camel from the Tang dynasty, a classical terra-cotta Greek head, and several Buddhas from the Far East. On the left side of the bookcase stood the Egyptian warrior goddess Neith, a figure Freud found especially fascinating. The effect of all the antique art and the couch with its pillows and complexly colored rugs, like a barge for a journey through remote spirit realms, was to make the consulting room look like a shaman's lair. It was a mystical space, haunted by the past and alive with promises of revelation.

The study, next door to the consulting room where Freud lay, was the place where Freud wrote his books and essays and talked with visitors, often far into the night. This room too teemed with antiquities and also held Freud's library, about twenty-five hundred books. The volumes were in English, which Freud read and spoke fluently, in Italian and French and Spanish, as well as in German. They covered almost every conceivable subject, including religion, anthropology, and history. The library was full of literary works, with books by Goethe and Schiller, whose styles he greatly admired, as well as by Shakespeare and Milton and Mark Twain. Freud had collected numerous volumes on archaeology, which he followed with a passion; he once said that he had read more archaeological studies than works of psychology, which is entirely likely. Freud did not think much of psychology until he himself intervened in the field.

On the crammed bookshelves, Freud had posed photographs of some of the women in his life. Freud and Martha stopped having sex after the birth of their last child, Anna, and Freud became a grand celibate, though a celibate intensely steeped in eros. Freud displayed a picture of Lou Andreas-Salomé, the most notorious woman in the intellectual world of nineteenth-

and early-twentieth-century Europe. Rilke and Nietzsche had both courted Lou, and Nietzsche, who did not generally think much of women, went so far as to ask Lou to marry him. Lou eventually became a disciple of Freud's and an analyst as well. Of Princess Marie Bonaparte, Freud had two photographs. "Our Princess," as Freud often called her, was a descendant of Napoleon, and like Lou had become a practicing analyst. It was to the princess that Freud had addressed his most famous query: "The great question which has never been answered," Freud said to her, "and which I have not yet been able to answer, despite my thirty years of research into the feminine soul, is 'What does a woman want?'" The third member of Freud's erotic trinity was the Parisian singer and actress Yvette Guilbert, another beauty, famously painted by Toulouse-Lautrec. Freud, who did not often go out, always did what he could to attend her concerts when she came to Vienna.

The center of the study was Freud's desk, where he usually sat after a day of seeing patients, smoking—for he could not think without his cigars—and writing his essays and his books in longhand. At the desk was a strange modernist chair—it looks like a homunculus—designed for Freud by Felix Augenfeld. When he read at the desk, Freud had the habit of slinging his leg over the side of the chair and twisting himself around corkscrew-style.

On top of the desk would no doubt have been the manuscript of Freud's book on Moses, which he had been struggling for a long time to finish. Some years before, Freud had written a brief essay—its first publication was oddly anonymous—about Michelangelo's sculpture of the prophet. It was clear from the essay that Freud had some vital, but still undefined, connection with Moses that he wanted to work out. Now he was about two thirds of the way through his book, which was as bold and speculative a piece of work as he had ever attempted. Freud had spent his career saying things that the public did not want to hear, but perhaps nothing he had published was as potentially inflammatory as this volume—he liked to think of it as his "historical novel." He wondered if he would ever be able to finish this strange project, which might serve as something like an intellectual last will and testament for Freud, and for psychoanalysis.

On the front of the desk, facing Freud like a chorus when he sat there, were thirty-five or so more figurines, perhaps the ones that inspired him most. They varied in size from the height of Freud's fountain pen, which he employed constantly—during the good times, Freud often wrote for four or five hours a day—to the size of a large wineglass from one of the family cupboards, which he would hardly have used at all; Freud was abstemious, and in fact highly suspicious of intoxication, whether from alcohol, religion, or romantic love. Here Egyptian figures predominate: Osiris, Isis, Neith. Few cultures were more mysterious, their secrets harder to crack, than Egypt's, and that fact drew Freud's intense interest. Behind the desk, was an urn, a south Italian bell krater, from the fourth century B.C., depicting the god Dionysus, which in time would hold Freud's ashes.

*　　*　　*

When the Nazis arrived at the door, Martha did not feel it necessary to summon her husband from his rooms. She was prepared to deal with the intruders on her own.

Martha and Sigmund had by now been married for over fifty years. She had raised six children, attended them in their many illnesses, guided them through personal crises, and created a smoothly running domestic sanctum, where the Professor—as almost everyone who knew and admired Freud called him—went about his intellectual business unbothered. Martha was highly organized and punctual, rare traits in relaxed Vienna; her house was always clean; the meals came on time. She had been just barely pretty as a girl—Freud informed her once that she had no claims on beauty—and now was stout, rather bland in appearance, and deliberate in all she did. Martha lived to make Freud's work possible, but as to what that work was, she had virtually no idea. She read a little for pleasure—but only after dinner, when the day's chores were done—and never entered into intellectual conversation with her husband. That was the domain of his male friends, of Anna, and sometimes too of Martha's sister, Minna, who had more aptitude for such things.

After asking the Nazis to deposit their rifles in the umbrella stand, Martha asked them if they might care to sit down. This too they refused. As the Nazis began to search the house, Martha went off, fetched the household money, and placed it on the dining room table. "Won't the gentlemen help themselves?" she suggested, and this time the gentlemen complied. They also, it appears, got the passports of the entire Freud family.

Anna Freud, seeing that the household money wasn't going to be enough for the Nazis, escorted them to the safe and removed the contents, six thousand Austrian schillings. The raiders fell on it quickly and began splitting it up. All was going according to the Nazis' design, but then, as Ernest Jones tells it, something unexpected happened.

From his sanctum at the back of the apartment came Sigmund Freud. He tottered into the front rooms, bent and frail, and he looked at the Nazis. Or, more precisely, he gave them a version of the stare that he had used time upon time to put his antagonists in disarray. It was the stare that he'd employed to respond to bitter criticism of his work and the stare he'd used to extinguish flare-ups of rebellion among his followers. It was the stare that he used when, a psychoanalytic session completed, the patient issued a disparaging or a discouraged remark. Freud aimed his stare at the Nazis and, the story goes, they scattered like mice.

Ernest Jones refers to the stare as a look of Old Testament rebuke and Freud's look that afternoon perhaps was akin to the one that Moses gave to the Jews when he came down from Sinai with the commandments in his hands and saw them worshipping the golden calf. Freud believed that Michelangelo's statue depicted the prophet at precisely that moment. The statue was about prohibition and power. But it was about power of a contained sort: in Freud's interpretation, Moses never throws down the tablets in rage. He provides an image of contained, sublimated anger.

After the Nazis had gone, Freud asked Martha how much they had taken. When Martha told him, Freud, never at a loss, replied, "Hmmm, I have never gotten so much for a single visit."

Freud's American friends were now rallying around him. On the day the Nazis searched his home and the press, John Wiley, the American chargé d'affaires in Vienna, aware of the threat to all Viennese Jews, sent a cable to Cordell Hull, the American secretary of state. "Fear Freud, despite age and illness, in danger." Hull not only sent a copy of the message off to William Bullitt, Freud's collaborator on the Wilson book, in Paris, but he also spoke to President Roosevelt about the situation. The president of the United States then took the time to learn that Freud would be well received in Paris, by Princess Bonaparte, if the French would only issue him a visa. Roosevelt ensured that Hull sent a message to Hugh Robert Wilson, who was the American ambassador to Germany. The message read, in part, "Wiley reported in a telegram from Vienna yesterday that he fears that Dr. Freud despite age and illness is in danger. The President has instructed me to ask you to take the matter up personally and informally with the appropriate officials of the German Government and desires you to express the hope that arrangements may be made by the appropriate authorities so that Dr. Freud and his family may be permitted to leave Vienna." Soon Cordell Hull knew that Freud's house had been invaded, his money stolen, and his passport confiscated, which only caused the Americans to step up their efforts to help.

Ernest Jones was as active as the American diplomats in the struggle to assure Freud's safety during the early days of the Anschluss. Jones—who had shown up at the Verlag to try to assist Martin, and then later saw the Nazis scurrying in disarray at Berggasse 19—was, aside from Anna, Freud's closest disciple. In his photographs, Jones cuts a rather elegant figure; he can look like a smooth Chicago gangster, one of Capone's lieutenants. He had a determined, manly face, with a prominent nose, and brought with him an aura of businesslike capability that seemed almost American. Early in his career, Jones had to leave England, where he was born, because he was accused of indecent behavior with child patients. Jones, for his part, argued that they were projecting their own fantasies onto him. From England, Jones went to Toronto and began to lecture on psychoanalysis. In 1911, he contributed to founding the American Psychoanalytic Association. Two years later, Jones returned to England and began practicing analysis.

Freud never had a more loyal follower than Ernest Jones. Though he disagreed with Freud on one or two matters, saliently on female sexuality, Jones invested himself completely in Freud's genius. Jones was a superb organizer, excellent at putting together conferences and at getting psychoanalytical work translated and published. But as Jones admitted time after time, he was not an original thinker. He defended Freud; he elaborated Freud's ideas, but he had little of his own to add. He seemed to want to guard Freud in the way that Huxley, Darwin's bulldog, guarded the intellectual legacy of the great theorist of evolution. Jones was constantly letting Freud know who was king and who was merely a servant to the cause. In a letter to Freud he wrote that "the originality-complex is not strong with me; my ambition is rather to know, to be 'behind the scenes,' and 'in the know,' rather than *to find out*. I realize that I have very little talent for originality; any talent I have lies rather in the direction of being able to see perhaps quickly what others point out: no doubt that also has its uses in the world . . . To me work is like a woman bearing a child; to men like you, I suppose it is more like the male fertilization." Then Jones, true to form, apologized for the style of his genuflection. "That is crudely expressed," he said, "but I think you will understand what I mean." Jones was tireless in Freud's cause; he was tireless in general. Having fulfilled his duties as Freud's intellectual defender, he found time to write a treatise on one of his favorite diversions, ice-skating. (In it, he recommends practicing in one's bedroom, surrounded by an ample supply of cushions.)

There were few people now in Vienna who could do more for Freud than Ernest Jones. But if Freud were to survive the occupation, he needed help not only with the Nazis, but also in overcoming his own feelings. When Jones sat down with Freud after the invasion of the Verlag and of Berggasse 19 and began to talk with him about leaving Vienna, it became clear that Freud was determined to stay. Jones insisted that Freud was not alone in the world, that there were many people who cared for him and who badly wanted him to live. "Alone," Freud answered. "Ah, if I were only alone I should long ago have done with life." Freud was sick of living for other people; he was tired and might not at all mind making an end to things. He told Jones that he could never travel; that he could not manage to make his way onto a railway compartment; and that, moreover, no country would be likely to take him. Jones countered that France might and that England probably would. Freud, pushed to the limit, told Jones that if he left Vienna, it would be much like the captain of a ship abandoning his post. Hearing that, Jones told the story of the second officer of the *Titanic*, a man named Lightoller. Lightoller was blown to the surface of the ocean when the boiler exploded on the ship and accordingly survived the wreck. He was interrogated afterward and asked, "At what moment did you leave the ship?" He answered, "I never left the ship, Sir; she left me." So Austria had detonated and ceased to exist. Freud would not be leaving Austria; Austria had left Freud.

Maybe. Maybe after a lifetime of Freud telling Jones what to do and (by and large) what to think, Jones finally took charge. Stranger things have happened. But it's much more likely that the events of Tuesday, March 22, which was to be one of the worst days in Freud's life, were the main influence on Freud's plans. By that bad day, though, the day that he almost lost Anna, Freud would have another ally, Ernest Jones's equal and perhaps more than that, on the scene.

This was Princess Marie Bonaparte, the woman Freud referred to as "our Princess," and whose two photographs were on display in his study. The princess was a descendant of Napoleon, a great-granddaughter of his brother Lucien. She was also married to Prince George, who was the brother of Constantine I, the king of the Hellenes, and first cousin to Christian X, king of Denmark. The princess was extremely rich and knew everyone in Europe, or at least everyone of a certain class. In her youth she had been a spectacular beauty, with many lovers.

Now in middle age, she was an impeccably handsome woman and relentless in her devotion to Freud. He had analyzed the princess, spending two hours a day with her, over a two-month period. Freud hadn't been able to solve the princess's sexual problems—she described herself as "frigid"—but by the end of the analysis, she had developed the power to work in a focused, productive way: the "energy devil," Freud came to call her. She became an analyst herself, wrote multiple papers and books, including a detailed study of Edgar Allan Poe, corresponded constantly with Freud, sent him money to bail out the always precarious Verlag, and generally used all her resources in the interest of the Professor and his cause.

The princess was smitten by Freud from the first time that she met him. She told him that he combined the powers of Einstein and Pasteur. "Do you really think so?" said Freud. "I'm very flattered. But I can't share your opinion. Not that I'm modest, no. I have a high opinion of what I have discovered, not of myself. The great discoverers are not necessarily great minds. Who has changed the world more than Christopher Columbus? Now who was he? An adventurer."

Freud was taken with the princess as well. He informed her that she was bisexual and could see the world through a man's eyes as well as a woman's. "Lou Andreas-Salomé," he told the princess flirtatiously, comparing her to the most seductive woman in the intellectual life of nineteenth-century Europe, "is a mirror—she has neither your virility, nor your sincerity, nor your style." The princess, Freud proclaimed, had "no prudishness whatsoever." Then Freud said, "Nobody understands you better than I. But in my private life, I am a petit bourgeois. . . . I would not like one of my sons to get a divorce or one of my daughters to have a liaison." Later, the princess recalled, "I dared to say to Freud that he must have a supernormal sexual development." "Of this," Freud told her, "you will not learn anything; perhaps not so super."

About his financial desires, Freud was much more forthcoming than about his erotic ones. He told the princess how he had lost his entire life savings in 1918: 150,000 crowns invested in Austrian state bonds, and 100,000 in life insurance. "He too little, I too much," the princess wrote in her journal, brooding on Freud's money woes. "Would he keep me [as a patient, as a friend] if I were ruined?"

Freud certainly would have. He respected the princess, liked her, and was drawn to her erotically, in his own peculiar way. The only occasions he seems to have shown prolonged impatience with her was when she insisted on having a pair of operations to move her clitoris closer to her vagina, the better to achieve arousal. (The operations did not work.) A few days after the Anschluss, the princess came to Vienna, took up residence at the Greek legation, and began eating meals with the Freud family. Like Ernest Jones, she was ready to do absolutely anything that could be done to protect Freud from the Nazis. And in 1938, when the Nazis were just making their way to international power, a figure like the princess could actually intimidate them. Her money and her lineage impressed them and she could, at least for the present, stand up to them with relative impunity.

On March 17, the day that the princess arrived at Berggasse

19, Hugh Robert Wilson reported that he had been in touch with German state secretary Ernst von Weizsäcker of the Foreign Office and had let them know about his concern for Freud. "I told him that I had received a telegram from Washington informing me that Doctor Freud, now an old man and ill, was desirous of leaving Vienna with his family for Paris, where he has friends who could take care of him. I added that he was widely and well known in the United States and that a permission accorded to him and his family to leave could not but create a favorable impression upon American opinion." Weizsäcker told the ambassador that he would do what he could.

But the person who may have had the most to do with Freud's eventual fate in Vienna was neither Jones nor the princess, nor any of the members of the American diplomatic corps, but a much more enigmatic figure, Doctor Anton Sauerwald. After the Anschluss, the Nazis appointed what they ingenuously called a "commissioner" for every Jewish business in Vienna, and Sauerwald was the man responsible for Freud and for the psychoanalytic publishing house. Sauerwald was thirty-five years old when he took charge of liquidating the Verlag's assets and turning them over to the Nazi government. He had been a student of science, medicine, and law at the University of Vienna and had graduated in 1929. Soon afterward, he went into business for himself, opening up a chemical laboratory in Vienna.

In the mid-thirties, Sauerwald played two roles. The Austrian government hired him to investigate and report on the numerous terrorist bombs going off in and around Vienna, many of them planted by the then-outlawed Nazi Party. (Sometimes as many as forty bombs a day went off.) This Sauerwald did with remarkable success: he was very quick to submit reports on the kind and amount of explosives used. Over time, he gained a stellar reputation with the Viennese police force for the accuracy of his reports. But this was only so because Sauerwald was manufacturing the explosives for the Nazis in his own laboratory. He built the bombs in the afternoon and reported on them the next morning.

When Sauerwald first took on the oversight of the Verlag, he comported himself like a fierce and dedicated Nazi. He insulted the staff, and in particular the gentiles who worked for the press, asking them again and again what they were doing consorting with Jewish swine. Sauerwald swaggered, fired invective, but in time he grew bored. And then he did something unexpected: he sat down and began to read Freud's books and papers at the Verlag. In them, he discovered some things that surprised him a great deal.

On Tuesday, March 22, the Gestapo came to Berggasse 19 and took Anna. They were persuaded that the International Psychoanalytic Association was a front for some antifascist political movement. Surely the person they most wanted to arrest and question was Freud. Anna told them that it was not possible for her father to leave the apartment building because he was ill and too frail to manage the stairs. She was willing to go in his place and to answer any questions the Gestapo might have about the association, as was Marie Bonaparte, who was also there in the apartment that day. But even though the princess asked to be arrested, the Nazis refused to take her, perhaps not wanting to risk the publicity that would come their way from arresting a royal personage. They were willing, though, to take Anna. Before she left with them, Max Schur, Freud's personal physician, gave her Veronal, a poison that would have allowed her to kill herself if the Nazis decided to torture her. Freud did not know about the Veronal, and if he did, he would no doubt have been enraged at Schur. But mostly now he was furious at the Nazis. All over Vienna, Jews were disappearing: some were killed, many were taken off to the concentration camp at Dachau.

The first thing that Anna did was to keep her head. Her brother Martin remembered her leaving with complete composure. He recalled "Anna being driven off in an open car escorted by four heavily armed S.S. men. Her situation was perilous; but far from showing fear, or even much interest, she sat in the car as a woman might sit in a taxi on her way to enjoy a shopping expedition." Soon Anna was being questioned at Gestapo headquarters.

No one now knows for certain what Anna said or did not say in her encounter with the Nazis. But she had observed her father well over the years, and he had provided her—just as he had provided himself—with something close to a perfect cover story to use in case of this kind of emergency. When the officers asked her if her father was political or subversive, or if any of his ideas might be an affront to the Reich, Anna had a whole grammar and vocabulary of response at her disposal. This language of exculpation was both radically misleading and absolutely true.

My father, she might have said, has always involved himself in science. He has labored for years in conditions as close to laboratory conditions as he can find in order to draw valid conclusions about the dynamics of human behavior. He has tried to write up these conclusions in dispassionate, clear language. Some of the conclusions, to be sure, are provisional, but, as he has himself said many times, he is waiting for further developments in biochemistry to confirm, or perhaps to modify, what he has learned.

Moreover, my father is a medical doctor with impeccable credentials. He is licensed to practice, to heal the sick, and he attends particularly to the sick no one else can help. He has taught at the university. He holds the rank of Professor.

As to day-to-day politics, they hardly interest my father at all. He reads the newspaper as others do; he follows events. But he is far too old, at eighty-one, and he is far too sick—his jaw has been operated on time and again for cancer—to be a rabble-rousing Austrian nationalist. When the Great War came in 1914, he dutifully sent his sons off to fight; he hoped for their safety and he hoped for the victory of Austria-Hungary and of its ally, Germany.

Granted, my father is a Jew, as I of course am myself. But Papa's commitment to Judaism has never consisted of much more than going to the B'nai Brith every couple of weeks and playing a spirited game of Tarok with other old men. He is not a Zionist and he is no Jewish rebel. And as his writings will show you, should you chance to read them, he is anything but a

Communist. Though it is true, my father will never deny his Jewish heritage. He is above all things an honest man. When he is healthy, he leads a regular life: breakfast and his patients; dinner, his walk, his beard trim, his paper, more patients; supper with the family, then work, work, late into the night.

My father has worked ceaselessly his whole life and over time this work, which is, as I say, of an impeccably scientific nature, has won him many admirers and many friends, some of whom do not lack influence in the world. He is an aged, peaceful, and overall harmless man, but, with all respect due, one would not lightly disturb the tranquility of what are almost certainly his final years. For such a disturbance would not be without consequences.

At home, waiting for his daughter, Freud paced the floor and smoked one forbidden cigar after the next. He did not speak; he was too distressed to utter a word, and he knew that nothing he could possibly say there in the front room of Berggasse 19, with his family around him, could have been of any actual help. Freud was an instinctive pragmatist in his external life: if something did not advance his cause, he did not do it. So there was nothing to say. But surely during those bad hours, Freud thought a great deal. Anna was so much to him. She was his intellectual confidante: Freud never wrote down an idea now that he not had tried out on Anna, discussed with her. She was his hope for the future. She was also his nurse and in this their relations were painfully intimate. Anna was the one who helped him take out the enormous prosthesis—"the monster" was what they called it—that sat in his mouth like a stone. She knew the harsh secrets of his old man's body, blighted by disease, and still loved him without qualification. Could he live in the world without her any longer than old Lear could after he lost Cordelia? Would Anna come no more—never, never, never?

At Nazi headquarters, Anna was no doubt telling the most blandly respectable story she could about her father—and he had left her plenty of resources to do so. But she might also have been thinking more candidly about the bearing her father's work actually had on the Nazis.

My father, she might have thought, as the dull questions came and came again, knows you far better than you know yourself. For years he has been writing about your ridiculous leader—the half monster, half clown—and all the others who've come before and all who will come later in his image. (For the hunger for this kind of man will last for all time.) He knows why you need the leader the way you do. He sees the God-shaped hole in your heart. And here is the strange thing: he sympathizes with the need. He knows it not to be alien but all too human.

To him, Hitler is not a special invention of the Germans, not their unique contribution to the world. My father understands that your Hitler is what everyone, man and woman and child, pines after. He is the answer to almost every human question, just as he is the destruction of everything that makes being human worthwhile. All the fiery joy you felt when you saw the glorious führer ride in state through Vienna—the apotheosis of the will—my father has foreseen. You are nothing new and wonderfully rebellious, as you imagine, but part of the endless recurrence of the same sad hunger for Truth, the Center, the King, and the Law. By understanding as much and making it plain for all who care to see it, my father is the one who has brought something new into the world.

It's possible that there was some intervention on Anna's behalf, perhaps help from the American embassy. Anna recalled a phone call that seemed to change the atmosphere. It could have come from the Americans; it could have come from Italy. Edoardo Weiss, an Italian analyst who knew Mussolini, said that Il Duce had intervened personally on Anna's behalf. Four years earlier Freud actually inscribed a book to Mussolini; it was the volume *Why War?* which Freud and Einstein authored together. The dedication ran as follows: "From an old man who greets in the Ruler the Hero of Culture." (In all probability what Freud was referring to in the dedication were the archae-ological excavations Il Duce was sponsoring in Italy, which Freud, as a student of past civilizations and past architecture, greatly valued.) It seems clear that if Mussolini actually read the book, he was not taking it to heart. In all likelihood, it was Anna herself who worked her way out of the Nazis' trap. More and more the Nazis were realizing how little the world cared about what was happening in Austria and how much they could do as they pleased. In significant matters they were becoming ever freer to make up their own minds.

At home Freud walked and walked, smoked and smoked. At noon he could not eat. He did not acknowledge anyone and said nothing. When Anna finally walked in the door early that evening, exhausted from her ordeal, the restrained Freud did something, we're told, that almost no one had ever seen him do. Sigmund Freud showed emotion; the great stoic may even have wept.

Perhaps it was during the black days around the time that Anna was arrested that Freud went furthest in considering suicide. His thoughts about suicide took two forms. The first was quite overt: the whole family might do what a number of Jews throughout Germany and Austria were doing, administering poison to themselves (Freud was a medical doctor after all; he knew something about making the matter as painless as possible) and so leaving the world that Hitler and the Germans were creating. But though Freud considered this option, he finally came out strongly against it. When Anna brought the matter up, Freud answered, with exasperation, "Why? Because they would like us to?"

Freud might also have committed a different kind of suicide, simply by staying where he was, refusing to budge. Freud and his entire family could easily have been taken off to Dachau and murdered. Yet Freud, old and sick as he was, could nonetheless be spurred on by Jones and by the princess, by the future of the psychoanalytical movement and by the prospect of one more battle in his long war with tyranny. The Moses book was still unfinished; the crucial third chapter, where Freud could add an installment to his critique of perverse authority and its uncanny appeal, still had to be finished.

There was also the fact that Freud had a very clear idea of what suicide was: he had written perceptively about what drove people to what Hamlet, the literary character who probably fascinated him the most, calls "self-slaughter." In "Mourning and Melancholia," Freud suggests that the main cause of suicide is an internal imbalance in the psyche. The over-I has become too strong, at the expense of the poor, depleted ego. The internal agent of authority rails at the self for its manifold inadequacies. But only when the ego is weak and unable to defend itself does it surrender to the over-I and do away with itself. If Freud were to commit suicide, overtly by taking poison, or covertly by staying put and letting the Nazis do as they would, he would be showing weakness. He would be showing that his sense of self, or ego, his confidence in who he was and what he had achieved, was not strong enough to fight against whatever forces were telling him that life, *his life*, was not worth living. He would, perhaps, be surrendering to the Nazi version of who Sigmund Freud was—a troublemaking Jew who'd written noxious books. "After the destruction of the Temple in Jerusalem by Titus," Freud told his Viennese colleagues at the meeting on March 13, the day before Hitler arrived in Vienna, "Rabbi Jochanan ben Sakkai asked for permission to open a school at Jabneh for the study of Torah. We are going to do the same. We are, after all, used to persecution by our history, tradition and some of us by personal experience." When he told his colleagues this, Freud was still not entirely determined to leave. But after the episode with Anna, Freud seems to have become convinced that the fight wasn't over and that he had something more to do in the world. Now, though, it was a matter of getting out.

On March 28, 1938, Freud and his family received good news. Ernest Jones had been in England, working on Freud's behalf, and he had gotten permission from the British government not only for Freud and his family but for others in the world of Viennese psychoanalysis to leave Vienna and to emigrate to England. In all, there could be eighteen adults and six children in the party—the number that Freud had insisted upon. Jones achieved this near miracle partly through the influence of his brother-in-law, William Trotter, who was the secretary of the Royal Society. Through Trotter, Jones got himself an introduction to the society's president, the physicist Sir William Bragg. Jones met with Sir William on March 23; Jones was taken aback, he said, to find out how naïve a distinguished scientist could be. When Jones told Sir William about Freud's plight, the scientist asked, "Do you really think the Germans are unkind to the Jews?" Yet whatever the limits of his moral imagination, Sir William immediately gave Jones a letter to Sir Samuel Hoare, the home secretary, endorsing Freud's case for immigration. (Jones already knew Hoare slightly: they belonged to the same ice-skating club.) Jones met with a member of Hoare's staff and two days later was able to write in his diary, "Saw Hoare's Secretary, A.S. Hutchinson, re Immigration. Success! First rain for 24 days. Amazing March."

England was willing to take Freud and his family but that did not mean the Nazis would be willing to let them go; there were still obstacles in the path. Most of the democratic nations were anything but hospitable to Jewish refugees—even those in a position to pay a high price for their freedom, as Freud and his family, with the help of Princess Bonaparte, were ready to do. Now, the Freuds would need to get the Nazis to issue an *Unbedenklichkeitserklärung*, a "statement of no impediment," which said that the government had no more claims to make on the family. To obtain the statement, the Freuds would have to pay a very large refugee tax, which would require Freud to liquidate many of his assets. Yet whether that, or anything else, would be enough for the Nazis was still open to question.

The Nazis had been aware of Freud's pernicious influence for some time. On May 10, 1933, young Nazis had broken into the main libraries of Germany and hauled out the works that Goebbels detested most. They brought the books out by carloads and set them on fire, chanting "*Brenne* Karl Marx! *Brenne* Sigmund Freud!" They burned Heine and Remarque, Mann, Zweig, and Gide. "This is a strong, great and symbolic act," Goebbels declared. "Never, as today, have young men had the right to cry out; studies are thriving, spirits awakening, oh, century, it is a joy to live!" Into the flaming pile went what were to become some of Heinrich Heine's most famous lines, "Wherever they burn books, sooner or later they will burn human beings also."

Before the Nazis took control in Austria, Martin Freud had shipped copies of his father's works away from the Verlag to Switzerland and presumed safety. But the Nazis found the record of the shipment and demanded that the books be sent back at the Verlag's expense. They were, and naturally, the Nazis destroyed them.

In the meantime, as the Freuds negotiated with the Nazi officials, Doctor Anton Sauerwald was growing impatient. The Freud case was moving slowly enough and his own political situation was still unresolved. During the days before the Anschluss, Doctor Sauerwald wore his Fatherland Front pin on the outside of his lapel, in apparent fealty to Schuschnigg and the party in power, while he wore his swastika on the inside, waiting for the great day to come. Sauerwald was devoted to playing both sides of the game, much as he was when he provided the Nazi terrorists with bombs *and* investigated their attacks on behalf of the police. Now, with the Nazis fully in power, Sauerwald was at a disadvantage because he could not claim the highly esteemed status of "illegal Nazi." That is, he had not made himself a member of the party before the Anschluss took place. The "illegal Nazis" were the ones who got preferment: chances for office, economic privileges, enhanced opportunities to loot their Jewish neighbors. Sauerwald applied to the party after the Anschluss, but was put on a waiting list because active recruitment was over. So Sauerwald sat and hoped for good news from party headquarters.

While he waited, Sauerwald read the works of Sigmund Freud. Virtually all that Freud had written on psychoanalysis was there to peruse, and as the long days passed, Doctor Sauerwald immersed himself. He had reason to be curious about Freud, not only because of Freud's notoriety in Vienna, but also because he had been a student of one of Freud's good friends, a Professor Herzig, who recommended Freud highly. So now Sauerwald was not only plunging into Freud's work, but also reading through all the private papers on file at the Verlag, among them papers that Martin Freud should have sent down through the intricate sewer system of Vienna.

During the days of March and April as he himself waited for news, Freud was not idle either. He was working on the Moses book, giving the project his most alert, composed hour each day. "Moses won't let go of my imagination," he had informed Arnold Zweig in a letter three years earlier, and it was still true. He would eventually tell Ernest Jones that his obligation to get the book written tormented him "like a ghost not laid." One of the things that drove him on was that in the character of Moses, Freud believed he could find the secrets of Jewish identity. "Several years ago," he observed, "I started asking myself how the Jews acquired their particular character, and following my usual custom I went back to the earliest beginnings. I did not get far. I was astounded to find that already the first so to speak embryonic experience of the race, the influence of the man Moses and the exodus from Egypt, conditioned the entire further development up to the present day." What Freud does not mention here, though, is that, to his mind, understanding Jewish character is integral to understanding human character and its promise for the future, however precarious such promise might be. For the Jews had given the world a great gift and also a great danger: the belief in an invisible god.

But during those weeks, Freud was also devoting time to

another literary pursuit. He and Anna were collaborating on a translation, from French to German, of Marie Bonaparte's book about her dog, Topsy. The book, which the princess published in 1937, was called *Topsy, chow-chow au poil d'or* (Topsy, the golden-haired chow). Freud was also a dog lover. Like the princess, he was devoted to chows, long-haired, handsome, highly intelligent dogs—"little lion-like creatures," as Freud's patient, the American poet H.D., described them.

Freud's first chow was Lun-Yug, who he acquired from Dorothy Burlingham, Anna's friend, in 1928. But after only fifteen months, Lun-Yug dropped out of sight in the train station in Salzburg while being taken to Vienna. A few days later, she turned up dead on the tracks. In March of 1930, Freud acquired his most famous chow, Jo-Fi (who was Lun-Yug's sister). Jo-Fi was Freud's constant companion, sitting at the foot of his consultation couch while analysis was in session, panting away rhythmically. Sometimes Jo-Fi received more attention than the patient. Said H.D.: "I was annoyed at the end of my session as Yofi would wander about and I felt the Professor was more interested in Yofi than he was in my story." Many patients noticed that the combination of Freud's cigar smoke and Jo-Fi's dog smell made the consulting room a place with a singular and memorable, though not entirely agreeable, scent. Bad smells or not, Freud adored his dog: after Freud underwent an especially painful surgery, he wrote to Marie Bonaparte, "I wished you could have seen with me what sympathy Jofi shows me during these hellish days, as if she understood everything." Freud's deep affection for dogs sometimes resembles that of his great precursor, Schopenhauer, who said that he would rather converse with his dogs than he would with most people.

Like Schopenhauer's, Freud's dog obsession probably arose in part from a mild misanthropy. (Hitler's dog obsession signaled a misanthropy that was not so mild.)

On January 11, 1937, Jo-Fi entered the hospital to have a pair of ovarian cysts removed. She came through the operation well enough, but on January 14, she died unexpectedly of a heart attack. Freud was crushed—"one cannot easily get over seven years of intimacy," he wrote to Arnold Zweig—and on the following day he acquired another chow, Lün. Originally Lün had belonged to him, but when it was clear that Jo-Fi could not deal with a rival, Freud packed Lün off to Dorothy Burlingham. In March of 1938, when the Nazis invaded, the beloved Jo-Fi was gone, and Lün reigned supreme in the Freud household. Freud greeted the manuscript of the princess's book about Topsy ("Teaupi" was the dog's formal name) with real delight: "I love it," he said. "It is so movingly genuine and true. It is not an analytical work, of course, but the analyst's thirst for truth and knowledge can be perceived behind this production, too."

About dogs, Freud had a very odd belief: he thought that they were creatures whose natures were entirely pure—untouched by civilization. Speaking of the princess's book, he said, "It really explains why one can love an animal like Topsy (or Jo-Fi) with such extraordinary intensity: affection without ambivalence, the simplicity of a life free from the almost unbearable conflicts of civilization, the beauty of an existence complete in itself. . . . Often when stroking Jo-Fi I have caught myself humming a melody which, unmusical as I am, I can't help recognizing as the aria from *Don Giovanni*: 'The bond of friendship / Unites us both.'"

The princess's book, highly impressionistic, sometimes operatic in style, was not the sort of thing that Freud was generally drawn to read. "Topsy," the princess cries at one point, "the greatest philosopher, strive as he may, will never know the visions which pass through your little golden head." Freud usually preferred his writers as tough, and relatively unadorned, as he was. But Freud adored this book and it was not only because of his affection for the princess and his love for chows, but also because of the story, which is the story of an illness. Like Freud, Topsy has cancer: both are afflicted with tumors on the right sides of their mouths. Like Freud, Topsy has surgery, and is treated, as Freud will be, with roentgen rays and radium. The princess was slightly embarrassed to take her dog to a clinic that was usually for people and dismayed at having to submit Topsy to the fierce regimen. But her love for the dog was so great that she went through with it.

The conclusion of the book is all that the princess—and Freud—might have hoped: Topsy is cured. "She runs along by the sea, inhaling the wind and the storm. Topsy, Topsy little healed dog, looking at you I am prouder to have almost magically prolonged your little life, than if I had written the *Iliad*." Topsy recovers; Topsy is alive and well after her struggle with cancer. She romps in the garden, she smells the ocean: Topsy is reborn. Freud, sitting with Anna in his study, going over their translation of the princess's book, had the chance to think about recovery and even perhaps about resurrection, albeit indirectly. Freud and Anna together, telling the story of Topsy, could brood on the possibility of more life.

"Does Topsy realize that she is being translated?" Freud

asked the princess in a letter. On April 9, the day that Adolf
Hitler returned to Vienna to begin building enthusiasm for his
upcoming Austrian plebiscite, Sigmund Freud wrote a simple
sentence in his journal: "Topsy translation finished."

For Hitler, in early April of 1938, things were going splendidly.
His success in Austria had enhanced his popularity even more
among the Germans. Middle-class nationalists, who before had
their doubts about Hitler, were now wild for him. In the
German army, where there had been skepticism about the little
corporal, there grew a sense that he was simply too popular to
oppose. Though quite a few members of the officers corps
believed that he was going to lead them all to ruin, they
concluded that there was nothing to be done about it, at least
for now. Hitler's speeches were full of celebrations of himself as
the man chosen by divine providence to lead Germany's rebirth.
He was so confident that he decided to go through with the
plebiscite on Austrian unification with Germany that Schuschnigg had scheduled for March 13, and that the invasion
canceled. The führer wanted to show the world that what he'd
done in Austria was entirely legitimate and that the Austrians
had embraced him as the figure of destiny he was.

On April 8, Hitler was back in Linz to campaign for the
referendum, and there appeared in the lobby of his hotel, Gustl
Kubizek, his best friend (and perhaps his only friend) from the
time when he was scraping by in Vienna before the First World
War. They had not seen each other for thirty years. The next

day, the friends had lunch together at the Weinzinger Hotel and they looked out the window at the Danube and the iron bridge across it, which Hitler had always detested. "That ugly thing, still there!" the führer groaned. "But not much longer, you can be sure of that, Kubizek."

What had happened to Kubizek since the war, Hitler wanted to know. Had he gone on to become a great musician, as he had hoped? Alas, Hitler's old friend was now a town clerk in Eferding, but there was a municipal orchestra and its program was ambitious.

"What, Kubizek," Hitler asked, "you even give symphonies in this little Eferding. But that's marvelous. Which symphonies have you played?"

Kubizek told his former roommate that they performed Schubert's Unfinished, Beethoven's Third, Mozart's *Jupiter* Symphony, and Beethoven's Fifth.

Hitler, whose love for art and music was undiminished, told his old friend that he would do what he could to help the orchestra. And what about Kubizek's personal life? Did he have a family? Gustl now had three boys, all of whom were interested in music.

"So you've got three sons, Kubizek," Hitler sighed. "I have no family. I am alone. But I should like to look after your sons."

Gustl told his old friend everything about his sons, two of whom were, as Hitler fancied himself to be, gifted draftsmen. Hitler listened intently and asked for every detail about the boys.

"I shall make myself responsible for the training of your three sons, Kubizek," Hitler finally said. "I don't want gifted young people to have such a hard time of it as we had. You know best what we had to go through in Vienna. But the worst time came for me later on, after we parted. Young talent must no longer be allowed to perish through sheer poverty. Whenever I can help personally, I do, and all the more when it's a question of your children, Kubizek!"

An hour later, Hitler left his friend and was on his way to Vienna to create the future for Kubizek's sons—whose musical education he did, in fact, arrange—and for the rest of the world besides. Again he was greeted by joyful crowds. The Nazis had transformed Vienna into a giant election theater. The trolleys were covered in red bunting with swastikas in front and on top, and everywhere there were placards proclaiming that Adolf Hitler was the man for Vienna—he creates work and bread. Party headquarters in individual districts were emblazoned with banners and slogans. In the Jewish quarter, Nazi flags flew everywhere and a huge banner shouted out the words "We remain true to the honor of our blood and give our voice to Adolf Hitler."

Saturday, the day before the plebiscite (and the day that Freud and Anna finished the Topsy translation), Hitler and Goebbels faced the crowd in Vienna. "Dr. Goebbels steps onto the balcony," a Nazi newspaper said, "and announces 'Germans, I proclaim the day of the Greater German Reich. Up flags.' Sirens howl. Flags rise on their masts. And the hundreds of thousands stand there with heads bared. Their silence is prayer. If we were asked to shout our joy out loud we could not. The tears running down the cheeks tell our creator infinitely more than storms of joy could say." Later that day, Hitler, comparing himself implicitly to Jesus, told the people how proud he was to have been born in Austria: "I believe that it was God's will to send a boy from here into the Reich, to raise him to be the leader of the nation so as to bring back his homeland into the Reich. Otherwise one would have to doubt God's providence." Close to tears, Hitler cried out to the crowd, "I believed in Germany at the time of its deepest humiliation."

Now it was the time for Austria to believe in Hitler. The next day, Sunday, came the plebiscite: In Austria, 99.73 percent of the voters approved unification. In Germany, 90.02 percent voted *Ja* and 99.8 percent approved Hitler's list of candidates for the new Reichstag. Only 11,281 Austrians voted against Hitler, 4,939 of those in Vienna. "For me," Hitler said, "this is the proudest hour of my life."

Many of the people who witnessed the events in Austria could not believe what they saw before them, an entire nation moving into barbarism. They believed that every monstrous step backward would be the last. And as a result, many of them stayed in Vienna and suffered the consequences. But Freud, again, had suggested why what was happening in Germany and Austria, as well as in Italy and Japan and Spain, might be close to inevitable. Freud, it is true, never applied his reflections to the immediate political situation in front of him, but he must have taken some dark, quiet satisfaction in having anticipated the horrible events at hand so well.

Fascism begins, Freud suggests, with the allure of the leader, the man of a masterly and charismatic nature who appears to be absolutely certain of himself and all that he does. However eccentric, volatile, and strange Hitler may have been in his private life—and he was all of those things—when he stood before a crowd, he was superb at playing the role. Here, finally, was a real man, a true force, all of whose energies flowed in one direction. But for Freud, the crucial question is why exactly the absolute leader should be such an important and, often, a necessary figure for human beings. Why did a figure like Hitler inspire such mad reverence?

At the center of Freud's work lies a fundamental perception: human beings are not unified creatures. Our psyches are not whole, but divided into parts, and those parts are usually in conflict with each other; for Freud the psyche is often in a state of tension that borders on civil war. The "it," or the "id," wants what it wants and does not easily take no for an answer. The over-I, or the superego, the internal agent of authority, often looks harshly upon the id and its manifold wants. The superego, in fact, frequently punishes the self simply for wishing for forbidden things, even if the self does not act on those wishes. Then there is the I, or ego, trying to broker between the it and the over-I, and doing so with the greatest difficulty, in part because both agencies often operate outside the circle of the ego's awareness. And Freud claims that the over-I can be unconscious, just as the it. Then too the "poor ego" must navigate a frequently hostile outside world. It is easy to see how, for Freud, life is best defined as ongoing conflict. In a well-known passage in *The Ego and the Id*, Freud observes that the ego is a "poor creature owing service to three masters and consequently menaced by three dangers: from the external world, from the libido of the id, and from the severity of the super-ego. Three kinds of anxiety correspond to these three dangers, since anxiety is the expression of a retreat from danger."

Humanity, Freud said, has come up with many different solutions to the problem of internal conflict and the pain that it inevitably brings. Many of these solutions, he believed, are best described as forms of intoxication. What the intoxicants generally do is to revise the superego and make it milder, less harsh in its judgments, and so more bearable. We like to have one glass of wine and then two, Freud suggests, because for some reason—he's not quite sure what it is in scientific terms—alcohol relaxes the demands of the over-I. "Why do we not get drunk?" Freud asked in a letter to his fiancée, Martha. The answer that Freud's later work suggests is because the pain that follows the next day is too hard to bear. This pain may not only be caused by the toxicity of alcohol, but also by the angry reassertion of the superego, which punishes the ego for deposing it and for acting (and thinking and desiring) in such shameful ways the night before.

Falling in love, claims Freud, and a thousand or so years of Western poetry, has a similar effect. Love—romantic love, the full-out passionate variety—allows the ego to be dominated not by the wishes of the demanding over-I, but by the wishes and judgment of the beloved. The beloved supplants the over-I, at least for a while, sheds glorious approval on the lover, and creates a feeling of almost magical well-being. Take a drink or two, take a lover, and suddenly the internal conflict in the psyche abates. A divided being becomes a resolved, unified, and temporarily, happy one. But these forms of inebriation have their built-in limits: after liquor comes the hangover, after love comes marriage.

Freud had no reservations about calling the relationship that crowds forge with an absolute leader erotic. (In this he was seconded by Hitler, who said that in his speeches, he made love to the German masses.) What happens is that the members of the crowd are hypnotized (and that is the word Freud uses) by the leader. The leader takes the place of the over-I, and for a variety of reasons, he stays there. What he offers to individuals is a new psychological dispensation. Where the individual super-ego is inconsistent and often inaccessible because it is uncon-scious, the collective superego, the leader, is clear and absolute in his values. He is associated with things that are permanent: with God, or destiny, or with absolute truth. He satisfies the human hunger to rise above time and chance and join with something more powerful and more enduring than merely transient, mortal enterprises. By promulgating one code, one set of values, the leader wipes away the differences between people, differences that can be a serious source of anxiety. Now everyone in Germany—and, the plebiscite over, in Austria as well—loves the fatherland, believes in the folk, blames the Jews, and has a grand imperial mission to fulfill.

But the leader is also permissive. Where the original superego prohibited violence and theft and destruction, the new super-ego, the leader, enjoins those things, though under certain prescribed conditions. So the day that Hitler arrived in Vienna, gentile Viennese, who had been so urbanely tolerant, could turn on their Jewish neighbors—and do so with a good conscience. When they broke into Jewish apartments and stole, when they trashed Jewish shops, when they made Jewish children scrub the sidewalks, they were doing two things at once: they were satisfying their most aggressive urges, and they were helping create a society based on higher values, one where the Jews were no longer in control. They did everything with a sense of righteous conviction: they were operating in accord with the new superego. All the energies that had been bound internally by normal human ambivalence could now be released. The anxiety that arises from both wanting to do something forbidden and not wanting to do it could be discharged. The result was a tremendous collective burst of passion—along with corresponding barbarism. Thus on the streets of Vienna, one saw in the new-formed Nazi mass exactly what Freud, in *Group Psychology*, predicted one would: "the weakness of intellectual ability, the lack of emotional restraint, the incapacity for moderation and delay, the inclination to exceed every limit in the expression of emotion and to work it off completely in the form of action."

Freud was no historicist and did not reflect on how some historical moments are more conducive to this sort of explosion than others. But it follows that when the world seems most disordered, incoherent, and inconsistent, and when humanity seems to be drowning in its own confusion, then the advent of a figure who can satisfy both the need for order *and* the need for indulgence is especially sharp. It was now such a time in Vienna. Just so, the last decades in Germany had been a time when Marx's phrase applied surpassingly well: all that was once solid had melted into air. As the historian Alan Bullock puts it, "Between 1918 and 1923, the German people . . . suffered a cumulative series of . . . shocks: defeat after the heavy losses of the war, Versailles, reparations, the collapse of the monarchy, revolution, near-civil war, and inflation. All the fears and insecurity of the postwar period were revived and made the harder to bear by the brief interlude of recovery, now [with the onset of the Depression] seen to be a treacherous illusion. In the early 1930s, millions of German men and women felt like survivors of an earthquake starting to put their homes together again, only to see the fragile framework of their lives cracking and crumbling around them a second time. In such circumstances human beings lose their bearings and entertain extravagant fears and fantastic hopes."

Freud tells us that we all long for inner peace. He says at one point in *The Ego and the Id* that it's probable that one of the reasons we need to withdraw regularly to sleep is that the work of maintaining the tensions within, among the various agencies of the psyche, is so taxing. When we sleep and dream, those tensions relax a little. But we want, quite understandably and also dangerously, to have the inner tensions dissolve not just at night but through all of our waking life as well. And we find dozens of ways to accomplish this. When we hear a joke or tell one, our forbidden desires break through, if only for the briefest moment. When we contemplate something beautiful, the tumult inside can still itself too. When we fall in love, when we play with a child, or (as Freud so much loved to do) pet a favorite dog, we experience a measure of inebriation. We get a little high. But that of course only sharpens our appetites to find a way to stay there, to get high and not come down.

We long, in particular, to replace our inconsistent, inscrutable over-I with something clearer and ultimately more permissive. We want a strong man with a simple doctrine that accounts for our sufferings, identifies our enemies, focuses our energies, and lets us indulge our forbidden desires with the best of conscience. This sort of man, appearing at the right moment, mouthing the right deceptions, rams life full of meaning and gives us, more enduringly than wine and even than love, a sense of being whole. Suddenly we are not at war within ourselves. The sense of anxiety departs and we feel free. The man who delivers this kind of intoxication must, as Freud says, appear completely masterful. He must seem to have perfect confidence, to need no one, and to be entirely self-sufficient. Sometimes this man will evoke a god as the source and guarantor of his authority, sometimes not. But in whatever form he arrives— whether he is Hitler, or Stalin, or Mao, or any one of their ilk past or to come—he will promise to deliver people from their confusion and to dispense unity and purpose, where before there had been chaos.

Easter Sunday, April 17, was the fifty-second anniversary of the beginning of Freud's practice as a psychoanalyst and it was a sad occasion, not least because Freud, who often thought of himself first as a healer, could no longer see patients. After the Anschluss, he dismissed his last two, finding it impossible to practice psychoanalysis because of the disturbances around him. "When the conscious mind is troubled," he said, "one cannot be interested in the unconscious mind." Freud had much to look back on in his career as an analyst but he must have done so now with some pain. Patients came to him, often in despair, because they were suffering and no one could help them. Faced with the neuroses, the average physician simply threw his hands up. Men and women who could not eat, who could not walk outside into the city square, who could not bear to be in a room with their mothers or fathers, who were so committed to ritual behaviors that they had no life beyond their sad obsessive acts— such people and many more like them made their way to Freud. He did what he could to acquaint them with the complexities of their desires and the strengths of their inhibi- tions. He told them stories about themselves that disturbed them dramatically—you're in love with your sister's husband; you wish your beloved brother were dead—and that they found disgusting, appalling. But then, over time, those patients often discovered that Freud had a point. They did desire forbidden things, but—as they also learned from the Professor—so did everyone else. Their desires may have been more potent than the norm, or their inhibiting energies might have surpassed those of other people, but the fact remained that there was nothing monstrous about them. "We are all sick," Freud used to say. Part of what psychoanalysis teaches is that there is no such thing as an original desire: Freud had seen it all before, or imagined it. He freed people so that they could bear at first just to glance at their strangest wishes, and then to stare with a spirit of calm toleration and even humor. Because of Freud the therapist, Auden said, "The child unlucky in his little State, / Some hearth where freedom is excluded, / A hive whose honey is fear and worry, / Feels calmer now and somehow assured of escape."

Surely Freud could be a dominating, even a domineering, analytical presence. The early case studies, in particular the stories of Dora and Emma Eckstein, sometimes make dispiriting reading. At one point in Dora's analysis, Freud, caught in what he would call the "counter-transference," the web of fantasies the analyst spins about the patient, concluded that what she wanted most was a kiss—and from no one other than himself.

Freud could also be dismayingly detached from his patients. Sometimes he was capable of suspending his belief that in analysis all was to be tolerated, and judged his more damaged patients as being barely worthwhile. The consulting room was Freud's laboratory and he occasionally regarded patients as though they were concentrations of data, fascinating data, to be sure, but no more than that.

Yet this condescension was infrequent for Freud the therapist. At his best, he saw himself as an educator. He taught people how to describe themselves in new ways. He helped them talk less moralistically and more tolerantly about themselves, and the result was to free them—sometimes a little and sometimes more than that—from their confusion and self-hatred. Overall, Freud loved his patients, though in his peculiarly severe way. That he no longer could see them surely left a void in his emotional life, as well as cutting him off from what was probably his major source of inspiration as a writer and thinker. Freud believed that neurotics extend and exaggerate normal human behaviors. They are not alien from the healthy ones. By seeing into neurotic patients, he believed that he could see into himself and humanity at large. Their sorrows were in a sense both his and everyone's.

It was not only patients that Freud was compelled to give up. On April 19, he gave his brother, Alexander, his stock of cigars. "Your seventy-second birthday finds us on the verge of separating after long years of living together," he wrote. "But the future, always uncertain, is at the moment especially difficult to foresee. I would like you to take over the good cigars which have been accumulating with me over the years, as you can still indulge in such pleasure, I no longer." Freud had been smoking since the age of twenty-four, beginning with cigarettes and moving quickly on to cigars. His father had been a heavy smoker, hanging on to the habit through to his eighty-first year, Freud's age when he gave his stock to Alexander. At the height of his commitment to tobacco, Freud was not only a user but a committed advocate. When his nephew Harry was seventeen, Freud offered him what would probably have been his first cigarette. The young man was judicious enough to refuse and Freud said, "My boy, smoking is one of the greatest and cheapest enjoyments in life, and if you decide in advance not to smoke, I can only feel sorry for you."

Freud called smoking "a protection and a weapon in the combat of life," and he was devoted to it for the great balance of his existence. When in 1923, he discovered a cancerous growth on his jaw and palate, he refrained for some time from letting his doctors know because he was aware that they would tell him that he had to give up his cigars. Freud did eventually let the doctors see the growth and they gave him the expected medical advice. But Freud being Freud, he ignored the doctors and went on smoking. At times his jaw became nearly frozen shut with pain, so Freud would use what he could to lever it open and insert his beloved smoke.

Cigar smoking gave Freud, who, despite an early fling with cocaine, almost never touched other drugs, the combination of energy and tranquility that he needed in order to write. Smoking calmed his nerves and let him focus his attention onto the field of inquiry at hand. His cigar unified him. When his onetime confidante Fliess convinced him to think psychoanalytically about smoking, Freud was compelled to admit that, like all addictions, cigar smoking was probably a substitute for the most common and most regressive addiction there was: masturbation. In all probability, Freud did not apply this diagnosis to himself. He was, he believed, a relatively sane man able to love and work—though over time it perhaps became clear to him that work was the thing that he loved most in life.

Committing oneself to smoking is a way to acquire a strong and persistent desire; because of tobacco's addictive power, the desire for it is nearly as potent as the desire for love or for fame. But the smoking desire can be met readily; the satisfaction of the desire to smoke depends by and large on oneself and oneself alone. Acquiring love or fame involves the capitulation of others. One needs a willing partner, an adulatory crowd. Freud's hunger for cigars was about as strong as any human hunger could be, and he himself was in control of satisfying it. "You actually do feel best," Freud's disciple Ferenczi once said to him, with a combination of admiration and concern, "when you can be independent of the whole world."

Even after he gave his cigars to Alex, Freud would continue to smoke. If food was the stuff of life, *Lebensmittel,* then cigars were to Freud "*Arbeitsmittel,*" the "stuff of work," and Freud, by his own estimation, still had a good deal of work to do. If he could somehow emerge intact from his encounter with Hitler and the Nazis, Freud had another struggle planned. This one was against a longtime adversary: Yahweh, God himself.

While Freud was surrendering his practice and at least pretending to surrender his dear cigars, Adolf Hitler was thriving. Elated by his victory in Austria, Hitler, who for a while displayed a genius comparable to Caesar's and Napoleon's for knowing the next move and when to make it, turned in a new direction: toward Czechoslovakia, an artificial country, an imposture created by the Allies after the First World War. The German General Staff had concocted a plan for invading the small nation—Case Green, it was called—but the plan had sat virtually unconsidered for more than two years. Now, seeing how smoothly things had gone in Austria, Hitler began to look for an excuse to invade. That was not hard to find: there were three and a half million Germans in Czechoslovakia, and they, as the Germans of Austria had done, were complaining ever more vehemently about persecution.

Hitler was still mildly afraid that France, England, and even the United States might intervene to stop him, so early in May, while Freud was waiting for his exit visa, and on the verge of celebrating his eighty-second birthday, Hitler went off to Italy accompanied by a staff of five hundred, all in uniform, to win Mussolini's blessing for the new adventure.

From Hitler's point of view, the visit to Italy was one protracted insult. He and the grand entourage were met not by Mussolini himself, but by King Victor Emmanuel. And Hitler was transported not in a motor car—he loved all modern conveyances and was ever ready to jump into an airplane, no matter what the weather—but in a coach drawn by four horses. At dinner, he was forced to accompany the queen, who towered over him, making him look absurd; she wore a crucifix around her neck, another attempt, surely, to diminish him. The king, for his part, spread rumors that Hitler was injecting himself with narcotics daily, and also that at bedtime he required a woman— not for any overtly sexual purposes, but simply to turn down the covers of his bed. Without this, the führer was purportedly unable to sleep. After an evening at the opera, Hitler appeared in public wearing a tuxedo, which was not, it seems, flattering dress for him. "The German Fuhrer and Reich Chancellor," one observer said, "looked like a headwaiter at the peak of business in a restaurant."

Mussolini stayed in the background, scheduling Hitler and his enormous party for one inane event after the next. But Hitler persevered. At last he made his way into Il Duce's company and managed to bring up the question of Czechoslovakia. Mussolini let Hitler know that the small nation was of no consequence to him, and that Hitler could proceed as he liked. As to the Allies, Hitler guessed that they were planning to do what they had done after each of his other bold moves: absolutely nothing. (He had taken to referring to the leaders of England and France as "the worms.") On this matter, as on many others that arose during the spring of 1938, Hitler turned out to be right. The British prime minister, Neville Chamberlain, wrote to his sister: "You only have to look at the map to see that nothing that France or we could do, could possibly save Czechoslovakia from being overrun by the Germans if they wanted to do it. . . . Therefore, we could not help Czechoslovakia—she would simply be a pretext for going to war with Germany. That we could not do, unless we had a reasonable prospect of being able to beat her to her knees in a reasonable time and of that I see no sign." Stalin professed endless loyalty to the Czech government, but what he truly wanted was for France and England to protect Czechoslovakia, not Russia. All of this Hitler quickly surmised. He had paid a price in humiliation during his trip to Italy—for which Mussolini would in time be compelled to pay—but now he was ready to expand the empire.

Freud's empire at the time was sickness and age and anxious boredom. While Anna and Ernest Jones and the princess negotiated with the Nazis, Freud sat and waited. He wrote an hour a day, working still on the Moses book; he read what he could; he tried to manage his correspondence; but mostly he waited and suffered. On April 26, Freud had an attack of deafness. For some time he had been having trouble with his hearing; postoperative infections had damaged his capacities on his right side, the cancerous side, so badly that he sometimes had to reverse the position of his chair to hear his patients. But now Freud's hearing faded out altogether for a brief span. It was perhaps fortunate that it did, for on May 1, Freud would have been compelled to hear the shouting in the streets that accompanied the Nazis' celebration. This was in all probability the day that the swastika went up over the exterior doorway of Freud's apartment, Berggasse 19, along with a banner that read, "The First of May shall document that we do not wish to disrupt but mean to build." The disrupters, presumably, were the Marxists of what had once been called Red Vienna; May 1 had been their day, the day that the workers massed to celebrate. Now this holiday, like everything else, was Nazi property.

On May 6, Freud, ill and disgruntled, marked his eighty-second birthday. Freud had never cared for his birthdays—they brought intimations of mortality—and was always at least moderately annoyed when the people around him made a fuss. Two years before, when Freud turned eighty, there had been a profusion of good wishes, which he had barely expected. When, in 1936, Ernest Jones told Freud that the British Psycho-Analytical Society was planning a major celebration for May 6, Freud told him that it made no sense to celebrate round-figure birthdays, especially when the person in question wasn't close to being intact. There was also talk about getting Freud the Nobel Prize for his eightieth year. That too irritated him: Freud, after all, was a renegade and renegades don't win major prizes.

But despite Freud's protests, eightieth-birthday salutations came to him from all over the world. He heard from Albert Einstein, Thomas Mann, H. G. Wells, Romain Rolland, Albert Schweitzer, and many others. Brooding on all the recognition, Freud wrote to Stefan Zweig that "although I have been uncommonly happy in my house, with wife and children and especially with a daughter who satisfied in rare measure all of a father's demands, I cannot reconcile myself to the wretchedness and helplessness of being old, and look forward to the transition into nonbeing with a kind of longing."

It is highly unlikely, though, that the birthday letter from Einstein failed to move Freud; for Einstein was what Freud often wanted more than anything else to be, a scientist. Einstein wrote to say that he had always been impressed by Freud's speculative power and by his cultural influence. However, he had lately come upon a case that brought home to him not only the intelligence, but the accuracy of Freud's way of thinking. "This gave me pleasure," Einstein said, "for it is always a source of pleasure when a great and beautiful idea proves to be correct in actual fact." Anna gave Freud her recently completed book, *The Ego and the Mechanisms of Defense*, in which he also took considerable satisfaction. Still, Anna could observe that, from her father's perspective, the best thing about the eightieth-birthday celebration was the fact that, eventually, it came to an end.

The coming of Freud's eighty-second birthday disturbed him yet more, so he decided to ignore it completely. To Ernest Jones, he wrote, "I am sitting here in my study being absolutely idle and otherwise useless. We have decided to disregard this birthday and to [postpone it until] 6 June, July, August, etc., in short, to a date after our liberation, and indeed, I have not acknowledged any of the letters, telegrams, etc. that arrived. Now it seems that we shall land in England in May after all. I say 'it seems' for, despite all promises uncertainty is the all-controlling factor." Freud's determination to get out of Austria was gathering force. To his son Ernst, Freud, not long after his birthday, wrote, "Two prospects keep me going in these grim times: to rejoin you all and—to die in freedom." To die in freedom: those words, written in English, declared Freud's developing allegiance to what he hoped would be his new home, and signified his deep determination to leave Vienna and Hitler, and with all the dignity that befit his age and his achievement.

Yet many members of the Gestapo had other ideas. All through Vienna, prosperous Jews like Freud were having their property confiscated and being taken off to Dachau, often with their entire families. Why should Freud be any different? In fact, his doctrines—"his obscene emphasis on sex" in particular—made him especially repugnant to the new regime. Why not create an example of Sigmund Freud?

At the Verlag, Doctor Anton Sauerwald, aspiring member of the Nazi Party, was making discoveries. He was reading Freud's work and finding out what a fascinating thinker the old man who had come under his charge was. And he was also discovering that he rather liked Freud: the Professor struck him as dignified, thoughtful, perhaps even brave. Sauerwald began to treat Freud and his family with a certain politeness. When a member of the Gestapo was rude to Freud, Sauerwald apologized later to Anna. "What do you expect?" he said. "These Prussians don't know who Freud is."

At the same time, reading through Freud's private papers at the Verlag, Sauerwald realized that Freud was breaking the law. He was keeping money stashed in foreign banks and not reporting it to the Nazis. The crime was punishable, at least nominally, by death. Surely it occurred to Sauerwald that if he reported Freud's financial situation, he would be able to advance his own fortunes; he could, perhaps, be officially inducted into the party. On Freud's birthday, May 6, the American ambassador to Berlin, Hugh Robert Wilson, reported to the secretary of state, Cordell Hull, that there was only one more matter to clear up, the settling of Freud's debts to the Verlag, before Freud would be allowed to emigrate. But that one matter was under the discretion of Doctor Anton Sauerwald.

A week after his birthday, Freud and his family received new passports from the Nazis. Their Austrian passports, which Freud and his family had used in the past to travel through Europe, were confiscated by the SA raiders on March 15, the day that Freud tottered out from the consulting room—the story goes—to scatter them like mice. But the old passports would have been no good anyway; they were Austrian and Austria no longer existed. The new documents that arrived on May 12 were German passports and bore the eagle and the swastika conspicuously on the front. In the passport photo, taken by Edmund Engelman, Freud wears a dark suit, with shirt and tie. Freud's shirt collar is loose around his neck, a sign that he had recently lost a good deal of weight. He looks overwhelmingly weary, and also mildly puzzled and mildly annoyed. He does not at all seem ready for a new start in a new country, a new life.

On May 5, Aunt Minna, ill though she was, had made her way to London; on May 24, Freud's daughter Mathilde and her husband, Robert, departed. On May 14, Freud's son Martin left Vienna for Paris, where his wife and two children had already fled. Though Martin had flushed many incriminating papers from the Verlag down into the Viennese sewer system, the Nazis nonetheless had left with a few compromising documents, probably about undisclosed funds of Martin's. It turned out that the vice president of the police, a man with an extensive criminal record of his own, was a good friend of Martin Freud's cook. Through the cook, Martin was able to buy back most of the documents, but apparently not enough of them. He soon learned that he was to be arrested; on Saturday, the fourteenth, he boarded a train for Paris.

Martin understood that it was forbidden to take any money out of Germany, so he sent back what currency he had and kept all of his coins in his pockets. But even that money might be too much. Martin was told that another Jew was recently taken from the train and shot for the crime of carrying a few stamps with him. Martin decided to take with him just enough money to buy food on the train.

After boarding, Martin went to the dining car and ordered up a whole roast chicken, asking the attendant to refrigerate it for him for the morning. "I filled that worthy . . . Nazi, with deep suspicion," Martin recollected. "He said the unusual request was a breach of customs regulations and that he would have to report me to the Gestapo." Martin canceled the request, took the chicken immediately to his compartment, and ate it all, while the dining car attendant watched from the corridor. As it turned out, there was no inspection at the border, and Martin Freud, stuffed with suspicious chicken, crossed the Rhine Bridge at Strasbourg unmolested.

Back in Vienna, Freud waited: he waited on the German authorities in general and without quite knowing it on Doctor Anton Sauerwald, who might at any time decide that it was in his interest, and the Reich's, to expose what he knew about Sigmund Freud. Though Freud had his passport, he also needed his "statement of no impediment," which indicated that all of his debts and taxes had been paid. On May 21, Freud received a statement about the value of his precious collection of antiquities, a statement that would be the basis for the tax he would have to pay to take them out of the country. The collection was valued—or rather, generously undervalued—at thirty thousand Reich marks; Hans von Demel, the curator of the Viennese Museum of Cultural History, had done Freud the good turn of pricing the antiquities at a low rate, so as to keep the tax on them within Freud's means.

Freud's obsession with his antiquities, never minor, had

increased that spring. He spent a good deal of time putting his books and statues in order, and he even began to catalog them—odd for someone as relatively unsystematic about such things as Freud was. One can only imagine Freud's thoughts as he went through his artworks for what he felt might be the last time. Creating the collection had been one of Freud's major avocations, even though he was always pressed for money and quite strict with himself about what he could and could not buy. One day a week, Freud held an open consultation period, when anyone who wanted to could come and get treatment or advice. With the money from those sessions, Freud pursued his passion.

Looking at the pieces now he perhaps recalled how he'd acquired each one and how much he'd paid. Freud was a very hard bargainer and knew the field well, so he was not often cheated. Probably too he thought a little about the authenticity of the work, for though he had a good eye, there were a number of forgeries on the market and in fact Freud did buy a few. (In the nineteenth and early-twentieth centuries, the sort of antiquities that Freud loved didn't generally command a high enough price to be worth forging.) Still he must have asked himself, Which are the most valuable? Which the most worth saving?

The antiquities had for many years been Freud's teaching tools. He told patients that the unconscious could preserve the past just as the dry sands of Egypt preserved this or that statue now standing intact on the bookshelf. Freud and the patient worked together to excavate the trauma or the dream and take it into the light of day, much as archaeologists dug deep for the treasures buried where ancient cities had been. Freud liked to tell his patients that a past memory, though as strange and disturbing as a statue of Toth was on first encounter, was nonetheless, like the statue, susceptible to analysis. What archaeologists and students of ancient history and religion could bring to understanding the icon, Freud and the new art of psychoanalysis might bring to interpreting a dream or a once-repressed memory.

But of course the collection had private resonances for Freud too. Many consequential thinkers and writers in the nineteenth century were drawn, as Freud was, to the pagan world and particularly to its religion and myth. One thinks of Nietzsche and his fascination with Dionysus and Apollo; Shelley and his great poem on Prometheus; and Keats in his ode to Psyche and the "Ode on a Grecian Urn," among many other writers. For these writers, pagan antiquity was a world beyond and before the Judeo-Christian world that they often found oppressive. By returning to the classical era, the poets and thinkers could reject the prevailing religious norms, but without surrendering to sterile skepticism. The pagan worldview allowed them to sustain their sense of wonder at the variety and strangeness of nature and at the miracle of their own being. Rome, as the formidable Edward Gibbon indicated, worshipped many gods, was hospitable to many religions, and that polymorphous worship was a source for the empire's urbanity and tolerance—and also for its amazing vigor. Perhaps Freud was one of that breed of modern pagans who would not give up pondering rich mystery, even as they repudiated the all-knowing sky god. The collection had been valued—good; there were promises that it would follow Freud into exile—also good. But surely the Nazis could confiscate it any time, prevent it from reaching him, if indeed he ever left.

Marie Bonaparte, who sat on the stairs every day after Anna was arrested to make sure that the Gestapo did not come and take away the Professor, and who often seemed to know what Freud needed, sometimes better than he knew himself, soon smuggled away his favorite treasure: a bronze statue of Athena, a little more than four inches high. Athena's left hand is poised to grip a spear, which was lost; in her right hand she holds a libation bowl. She is wearing a Corinthian helmet, set far back on her brow, and a breastplate, decorated with the figure of Medusa, though in this rendition, Medusa is without her snakes. The statue had a special place in Freud's heart, symbolizing both wisdom and martial prowess; it was an icon of the mind as warrior, the intellect combatant. Marie Bonaparte held it for Freud at her home in Paris to present to him when he was finally free.

Still Freud did not have his *Unbedenklichkeitserklärung*, the statement of no impediment. The Germans had put Freud in the same position in which they put many Jews: they took all he had on hand and then demanded that he pay taxes on it. They had seized the press, and they had seized Freud's Viennese savings. So they put Freud in an impossible situation. You must pay taxes and all of your supposed debts; but we've confiscated your funds. What will you do? The Nazis claimed that Freud owed a debt to his publisher, the Verlag, which was now in their hands: the sum was 32,000 schillings.

What Freud needed at this point was ransom money, pure and simple. The resources that he himself had had on hand were all but gone. Now Marie Bonaparte was compelled to do more than rescue the statue of Athena for Freud. Now she stepped in and paid off the criminals masquerading as officials, and finally, Freud seemed to be free to go.

Freud was far luckier than most Jews in Vienna. To reach the verge of emigration, he had the help of the American government (including President Roosevelt himself); the British government (which had to agree to accept him); his well-connected and wealthy friend, the princess; the analyst Ernest Jones, who was born for bureaucratic intrigue; intrepid and levelheaded Anna; his dutiful son Martin; and a dozen others.

Yet there was still one more factor: Doctor Anton Sauerwald. Anxious and unhappy, sitting in the Verlag, hoping to advance his career and become a figure of note in the new Austria, Sauerwald commanded the destiny of Freud and his family. All he needed to do to have them arrested was to reveal the information he had about the funds in foreign banks. There were figures high in the Nazi Party who reportedly would have been happy to do away with Freud, even now at this last minute. The story goes that Hermann Göring, whose cousin had taken over the Berlin Psychoanalytical Institute, supported letting Freud go. But against him were arrayed both Goebbels, the propaganda minister, and Himmler, who would in time be a key figure in implementing the Final Solution. A phone call to the office of either man, placed by Sauerwald, would almost certainly mean the arrest of Freud and his family.

*   *   *

On Saturday, June 4, Sigmund Freud boarded the Orient Express, with Martha, Anna, Doctor Josefine Stross, the housemaid, Paula Fichtl, and Lün, his chow. Doctor Stross was a late addition, for, as Freud said, "Dr. Schur, our family doctor, was to have accompanied us with his family, but at the eleventh hour he was unfortunate enough to require an appendix operation, with the result that we had to content ourselves with the protection of the lady pediatrician, whom Anna brought along." The train made its slow way across Germany and to the border of France, and Doctor Anton Sauerwald, for whatever strange complex of reasons, did not intervene. Whether it was loyalty or laziness or hopes for some later relations with Freud—in fact, Sauerwald would appear again in Freud's life—one cannot know. When the train crossed the Rhine River, Freud offered a simple remark, "*Jetzt sind wir frei.*" Now we are free.

Behind him, Sigmund Freud left Berggasse 19, soon to be empty of its furnishings, and the Verlag, stripped of its assets; he left Vienna, the city he both hated and loved, in the control of Adolf Hitler; he left four sisters, too old to travel, under the care of friends; he left a population of Jews that would soon be virtually destroyed; he left his life, his history, and the site of all of his major achievements. But he left something else, as well. Before Freud boarded the train, the Gestapo required him to sign a document. It said, "I Prof. Freud, hereby confirm that after the Anschluss of Austria to the German Reich I have been treated by the German authorities and particularly by the Gestapo with all the respect and consideration due to my scientific reputation, that I could live and work in full freedom, that I could continue to pursue my activities in every way I desired, that I found full support from all concerned in this respect, and that I have not the slightest reason for any complaint." Freud signed, but then he added one simple sentence: *Ich kann die Gestapo jedermann auf das beste empfehlen.* "I can most highly recommend the Gestapo to everyone."

There's brilliance, as well as a remarkable daring, in Freud's send-off to the Nazis. He offered them a statement with a latent and a manifest content, with a double meaning. And double meanings (and triple meanings and proliferating, complex meanings of all sorts) were precisely what Nazis were allergic to, what they had, in effect, constructed their world to shut out. To the Nazis, there always had to be one: one people, one nation, one leader, and one meaning, the truth. The Gestapo must have been most flattered by the old Professor's compliment.

Hitler, meanwhile, was thinking of Czechoslovakia, that small, abominable nation thrust like a fist into German territory. And the führer was continuing to reap the adulation of the Germans, and now too of the Austrian people. What he brought them, from the perspective of Freud's thinking at least, was an elixir like no other: he brought unity. People were divided in themselves; nations were split: the leader pulled all the achingly disparate parts together and dispensed a feeling of oneness. He healed the fragmented psyche—provided one did not wish to think for oneself, make one's own ethical judgments or interpret things in one's fashion—and he healed the broken polis, so long as one was not a Jew, a Gypsy, or a Christian who took too seriously the teachings of Jesus Christ.

While Freud can affirm, though not without a touch of irony, such mild intoxicants as love and art, he is nonetheless supremely suspicious of any doctrine or activity that promises to unify the psyche—or the nation or the people—and to do so for the long term. After alcoholic intoxication comes the hangover; after aesthetic contemplation, boredom; after the intoxications of romantic love, marriage. Love, art, and liquor are temporary ways of transcending the pain of being: they have limits built into them. But belief in the leader or in the one true God can continue on for a lifetime and sometimes then for generations.

Freud's implicit ethos in the face of the temptation that fascism and fundamentalism offer—the temptation of one-ness—is counterintuitive. He believes that the inner tensions we experience within the psyche are by and large necessary tensions. This is so not because the tensions are enjoyable in themselves—they are not—but because the alternatives are so much worse. It's true that when internal dissonance becomes too strong, the result is likely to be neurosis. When the drives are too potently controlled—Freud's term for this is "repression"—they will express themselves in indirect, painful ways. But complete unbinding of the inner tensions is worse: that leads the way to public and private chaos.

For Freud, a healthy psyche is not always a psyche that feels good. The tension between the agencies within is manifest as an anxiety that is very difficult for the individual to explain or to remedy. One never feels exactly right in part because, virtually all the time, one is indulging a certain powerful agency and neglecting the others. One is, perhaps, striving for success and, accordingly, placating the over-I. But at the same time one is outraging the it, which cries for pleasure, and overwhelming the I, which cannot, no matter how hard the over-I pushes, live up to its demands for achievement and success. Because a good deal of the psyche's business goes on unconsciously, and because the demands of the various agencies change over time, it is diffi-cult—perhaps it is nearly impossible—to follow Socrates' dic-tum and, with confidence, to know oneself. For Freud, the self is prone to oppose itself and often in ways that are simply incomprehensible to the individual. In one of the saddest sentences Freud ever wrote, he observes how someone suffering under an irrational sense of guilt becomes sick, but without knowing the source of his sickness. "As far as the patient is concerned," Freud writes, "this sense of guilt is dumb; it does not tell him he is guilty; he does not feel guilty, he feels ill."

But Freud also suggests that a measure of inner conflict is not the worst thing in the world: We need to learn to understand the conflict to whatever degree we can and perhaps modify it in certain ways. But overall we need to learn to see some inner tension as inevitable, and to live with it. Freud's view that we need to tolerate and even at times cultivate conflict is part of what makes his thought as radical as it is. Almost all other religious and spiritual traditions prior to Freud have held up inner peace as an ideal. Christianity celebrates peace above all things and tells its adherents to avoid war by forgiving their enemy and by turning the other cheek; Buddhism affirms the tranquility that meditation and detachment from desire can bring; the name Islam denotes peace; Judaism endorses the calm that attends on fulfilling the covenant with the Lord. There is room for turbulence in all these faiths to be sure: the Muslim enters spiritual struggle, jihad; the believing Christian wars against his tendency to sin. But ultimately the goal is to achieve inner union through the development of the spirit.

Jung once remarked that the objective of the yogi is to use breathing and postures, the asanas, to bring himself into a state of calm in which no material from the unconscious can penetrate the conscious mind. Such an activity is representative of a good deal of religious practice in both the West and the East. Prayer, fasting, meditation, penance, confession, chanting, song—all these activities can quell inner turbulence. But Freud affirms not inner peace but inner conflict. No part of the psyche must be suppressed in the interest of any other; the wages for such suppression are too dear. Any part of the self denied expression is bound to erupt—or at least to assert itself—in ways that will be harmful for the individual. "The mind," as Emerson says, "goes antagonizing on."

Just as a healthy psyche is not always a serene psyche, so Freud implies that a healthy body politic is not always a tranquil one. A healthy political society is one that allows for a good deal of ongoing tension. When the people surrender their will to the leader, as the Germans and, rather shockingly, the Austrians did to Hitler, the result is a certain sort of peace of mind. One wakes up with a sense of purpose: all the energies stream in the same direction; the world is a much clearer and simpler place. "The masses," Hitler wrote, "love a commander more than a petitioner and feel inwardly more satisfied by a doctrine, tolerating no other beside itself, than by the granting of liberalistic freedom with which, as a rule, they can do little, and are prone to feel that they have been abandoned." To be sure, living in a relatively liberal democracy, with its proliferation of ideas, interpretations, and values can be dizzying. There's a great deal of argument, controversy, difference. But in that difference, annoying and perplexing as it may be, lies the community's well-being. Freud suggests that if we are willing to live with inner tension, political as well as personal, we need never be overwhelmed by tyranny or fall into the anarchy that complete surrender to the unconscious brings.

Freud feared the United States of America as much as he did because to him it represented something like the dangerous inverse of Nazi Germany. Germany was insanely authoritarian. But America was dangerous because it always threatened to be dominated from below, by the appetites. (In his perception of democracy Freud resembles Plato, who in *The Republic* associates the rule of the people with the unqualified rule of the desiring, or appetitive, part of the soul.) Aggressive democracy, to Freud, meant discrediting all leaders, no matter how sane or useful, and allowing the majority to dominate completely. Freud knew how difficult it was to sublimate the drives—to turn erotic and aggressive energies to the interest of civilization. Most people wanted satisfactions that were crude and immediate. They would not wait, as the truly civilized man or woman does, to have their efforts repaid. A society that merrily disregards all leaders, the insane and the benevolent alike, is going to devolve into chaos—and this is what Freud expected to happen at any moment in America. The only thing that saved America, as Freud saw it, was that its people burned off most of their potentially destructive energy in the quest for wealth. But when that quest was comprehensively thwarted—as the Depression of 1929 threatened to do—then Americans could easily and readily turn to anarchy. When Freud thought of relatively free and enlightened nations, he thought of France and, above all others, of England, the country he revered from his young manhood on, and to which he was now, at last, making his way.

John Keats reflects in a letter on Adam's dream: "He awoke and found it truth," the poet says. The dream that the first man dreamed was of a beautiful lover and helpmate: he dreamed of Eve and woke up to find her there beside him. Freud had dreamed a dream as well: it was a dream of a world dominated by a primal man, a cruel half-mad figure of ultimate potency, worshipped by virtually all. What the primal man wants he takes; his whims, hateful as they may be, quickly translate into edicts and then into facts. Freud dreamed that dream and, like an accursed Adam, woke up and found it true. The world he had lived and thrived in was indeed dominated by such a man. And this happened not when Freud was twenty-five or fifty, when he might have had plentiful resources to fight back, but when he was in his eighties and very sick.

Yet while Hitler and his minions dominated the streets of Vienna, Freud labored for an hour a day on his Moses book, a book that he hoped would stand as part of his twenty-year analysis of the kind of debased authority that Hitler represented. If Freud's ethic might be called an ethic of civilized strife, then during his last days in Vienna he lived up to it in many ways. It was not easy for an old man to stand up to the Nazis, to strive with them. Nor was it easy to continue working away on his book, which, Freud often admitted, he wrote against multiple inner resistances.

But Freud was also willing to play a little bit. He could relax enough to sit with Anna and to translate, not a major work of literature, a tragedy by Sophocles or by Shakespeare, but a book about a dog. "Does Topsy realize that she is being translated?" Freud asked the princess. Well, Topsy was. During the perilous three months in Vienna, Freud, though old and ill, was in many ways at his height. He did his work, he cared for his family, and as well as he could, he sustained his spirits. He never lost his wits; nor did he—"I have never gotten so much for a single visit"; "I can most highly recommend the Gestapo to every-one"—ever lose his wit.

Yet there is more to the story. In his great elegy for Freud, W. H. Auden saw how "the autocratic pose / The paternal strictness he distrusted, still / Clung to his utterance and features." Surely it did, and in Vienna during the last days, as it was through almost all of Freud's adult life, there was an element of that patriarchal character clearly perceptible. Even at his best, there is something stiff and overly commanding about Freud. He is stubborn, hyperconvinced of his own opinion, deaf to other views. Persuading Freud to try to leave Vienna and save his life and the life of his family was a major endeavor.

Emerson, in what was, presumably, a hyperbolic moment, counsels that we should pretend that the other people around us are real. Who knows? he asks himself. Maybe they are. Freud's behavior toward others can sometimes suggest that he nourished pronounced doubts about their actuality too. He was capable of comparing the prospect of Anna's moving away and abandoning him and Martha with his having to give up his cigars. Freud's treatment of his other disciples is a complex subject, but one could never mistake him for a humane and humorous, much less a loving, mentor. He sometimes appears to believe that his disciples were created for the exclusive purpose of developing his work and enhancing his reputation. Their vocation in life was to think Freudian thoughts that Freud hadn't the time or occasion to think, then to listen to the master praise them for being loyal, even as he subtly disparaged them for being unoriginal.

The fact is, of course, that in the middle of his career, Freud arrived at a strong view about the kind of authority that commands obedience: masterful, patriarchal authority. At various times in his life and work, Freud was willing to imitate exactly such authority: his temperament leaned more than a little that way to begin with, and he saw how effective it could be to play the primal father's role. Freud, in short, was tempted by the kind of power that he spent a major phase of his career demystifying. Freud, one might say, was a patriarch who worked with incomparable skill to deconstruct patriarchy. He wrote and lived to put an end to the kind of authority that he himself quite often embodied and exploited.

II

London

Early on the morning of Monday, June 6, 1938, Sigmund Freud stepped down from a train at Victoria Station in London. The train had pulled in to a far corner of Victoria so that Freud could avoid the crowd that was gathered to greet him. His escape had been reported in the British newspapers and there was great public enthusiasm about his arrival. Though the weather was mild, Freud wore a densely woven three-piece suit, a heavy topcoat, a fedora, and thick black shoes. He was frail from his illness and still weary from the trip, so he made his way down from the train with considerable difficulty. His expression was uncertain, at times even slightly disoriented. A chance observer, seeing Freud on his arrival in England, might have thought of some lines by the great Irish poet William Butler Yeats, who, in June of 1938, was also nearing his end: "An aged man is but a paltry thing," Yeats said, "a tattered coat upon a stick." Surely on that day in June, Freud looked paltry enough, a sad, diminished ghost of his former self.

As Freud stepped off the train, he might well have thought that his trials were over. But here in England, Freud would find a new set of adversaries, different but not entirely unrelated to those he left behind in Vienna. Freud, who had often been ignored and derided in his home city, would, in England, become an admired figure. And surely public acclaim was something that Freud had wanted all his life. Yet in order to live up to his own aspirations as a writer and thinker—and as an individual—Freud would have to contend against his newfound celebrity. He would have to fight against his own urge to become—Yeats once again—"a smiling public man."

Then there was the matter of death: Freud had come to England, he said, so as "to die in freedom." He was aware that the cancer of the jaw that had been with him since 1923 was going to kill him, and relatively soon. But how was he to die? The fact that the illness was gradual and protracted gave him some choice in the matter. Freud understood that his way of dying was bound to be of consequence, and not just to himself and to those close to him. Freud had invented psychoanalysis, but he also embodied it. People looked to him as an exponent of a set of provocative, controversial ideas, but they also saw him as an exemplary figure, one who, in some ways at least, attempted to live by the findings that he offered the world. Socrates, Cicero, and Montaigne all had said that to philosophize is to learn how to die. Freud's death would inevitably be a commentary on the philosophy of life that psychoanalysis offered.

Perhaps more than anything else now, Freud wanted his work to last. He wanted his thoughts to be part of the thought of the civilized future—even perhaps to dominate that future. Over the past twenty years, Freud had reflected continually on how authority establishes and perpetuates itself, and much of what he had concluded was disturbing. He knew, or thought he knew, that the world longed for father-gods, the more severe, inscrutable, and potent, the better. To pass out of life in the guise of such a figure might help to ensure Freud's future authority. But would dying as a "great man" not undermine what Freud had written about the need for liberation from all oppressive patriarchs?

Getting off the train that Monday morning, though, Freud was simply relieved to be in London, happy to be alive. If his dream life was any indication, he was looking to the future with some hope. The night before, as he crossed over from France on the ferryboat to Dover, Freud dreamed that he was landing not at Dover but at Pevensey. When he told his son about the dream, he was forced to explain that Pevensey was where William the Conqueror had landed when he invaded England in 1066.

As tired as he was, Freud insisted that he wanted to see something of his new home. So Ernest Jones drove him north, toward his new residence, through the center of London. As they made their way, Freud showed Martha the sights: Buckingham Palace and the Houses of Parliament, Piccadilly Circus, Regent Street, and all the other places, which he had read so often about and also recalled from his time in England. As he passed the palace, Freud perhaps reflected on the near-perfect political balance that England had achieved. Here was a monarchy to absorb the people's need for commanding, parental figures, father- and mother-gods. But the monarchy was largely ceremonial; the kings and queens had little power to deploy. Meanwhile, England was governed by its most able men, none of whom the crowd could ever elevate to absolute heights, for the beloved rulers were already in place.

On an average day, Freud would have seen as many as a half million people on their way to work in what was now the largest city in the world. By 1939, London's population would be 8.2 million. But today was Whit Monday, the day later known as Late Spring Bank Holiday, and most people had the day off. Freud, coming into London, saw a heavy flow of cars heading out of the city and off in the direction of the seashore. That morning, the beaches were filling with young girls displaying the latest fashion: silk or knitted Snow White hoods, inspired by the recently released Disney movie. On the day that Freud arrived, the film was playing continuously from eleven to eleven at the New Gallery. In London, over 61,000 people would use the holiday to visit the zoo at Regent's Park, while an annual parade of 574 cart horses took place nearby. Elsewhere in the park, Mozart's *Così fan tutte*, an opera which Freud quite liked, would play at an open-air theater, though mostly to empty seats.

Looking out the window of the automobile as Jones drove him to his new home, Freud saw a London that on this holiday Monday seemed relaxed and confident. Yet in Parliament the week before, all the discussion had been about war, and in particular, about what effect high-intensity aerial bombardment would have on the city. Members asked what London would do if the telephone system failed. They wanted to know what safeguards were in effect for the water supply and the gas and electric systems.

Surely the political event that most preoccupied Freud that day was the annexation of Austria, with the rubbing parties and break-ins and the horrors on the street. The recent occurrence that most transfixed Londoners was not the Austrian conquest—thought that was disturbing enough—but the bombing of Guernica. A Basque town in the north of Spain, Guernica had been attacked by German planes in April of 1937. The Germans, allied with Franco and the Spanish fascists, were using Spain to train their soldiers and to try out their new weapons, and at Guernica that weaponry succeeded beyond all expectations. The attack occurred on a market day, with everyone out in the streets, and resulted in a horrible slaughter of men, and of women and children as well. An "experimental horror," Churchill called the Guernica bombing. Picasso's painting of the attack—with people and animals emanating their inaudible, ear-splitting screams—over time became an emblem for the brutalities of a new kind of warfare in which the armies did little to avoid civilian populations, and in fact often sought them out for slaughter.

In the spring of 1938, experts were telling the British population that a hundred thousand tons of bombs would fall on London during the first fourteen days of a war with Germany. Every ton of bombs, they calculated, would result in fifty casualties, so the prospects were terrifying. Bertrand Russell, probably England's most prominent public intellectual at the time, wrote that "London . . . will be one vast raving bedlam, the hospitals will be stormed, traffic will cease, the homeless will shriek for help, the city will be a pandemonium." In fact, the total of bombs dropped on the city never reached a hundred thousand tons, and the casualties would prove to be much less than the experts predicted, though they would be grievous enough. When Freud arrived in London, the British, as preoccupied as they might have seemed with Snow White and beach holiday-going and the animals at the Regent's Park zoo, were in a state of fear, expecting that London could soon become Guernica on a grand scale, at least if Neville Chamberlain couldn't somehow arrange to placate Hitler. In June of 1938, Freud came to a London obsessed by peace and the appearance of peace and terrified by the prospect of war.

Freud was also arriving in a London that was unusually warm in its attitude toward the Jews. As a general rule, the British at the time had only a minimal interest in what went on in other nations—a post–World War I isolationism was potently intact. But that began to change when word of the way that the Germans were treating the Jews began to spread outside Germany and Austria. Up until this point, British culture in the twentieth century was mildly, but rather consistently, anti-Semitic. Jews were barred from golf and social clubs and the great public schools had strict quotas for Jewish admission. But Germany's Nuremberg Laws, with their restrictions on Jewish travel, marriage, and professional life, revolted the British and spread sympathy everywhere in the nation for the Jewish plight. As the historian A. J. P. Taylor puts it: "It was the [German] reversion to barbarism almost as much as the barbarism itself which made Nazi Germany peculiarly hateful, and some English people were no doubt the more annoyed at having to repudiate the anti-semitism which they had secretly cherished." Robert Graves and Alan Hodge put things more pungently. British fascists, they say, under the leadership of Sir Oswald Mosley, "tried to exploit anti-Semitic feeling in the East End, but with the surprising effect, rather, of making heroes of 'the kikes.'"

After taking in the London sights, Freud and his party stopped at 39 Elsworthy Road, the house that Ernst Freud had rented for his father and mother and Anna while the family looked for what would, in Freud's case, be a final home. Freud called 39 Elsworthy Road "a charming little house. My room," he said, "looks out onto a verandah which overlooks our own garden framed with flower beds and gives onto a large tree-studded park. Naturally it is only a temporary measure for three months. Ernst still has to find the definite solution which needs to fulfill all sorts of conditions which are seldom realized here. It is difficult for us to live vertically instead of horizontally." Gone was Berggasse 19, where the Freud family had lived its horizontal life; now, in a house with stairs, Freud would have to be carried from upstairs down to the main part of the house. Still, Freud found the new house appealing. The *Daily Herald*, which took a keen interest in Freud's arrival, described Freud's new residence as "a quiet, spacious modern house with a vivid green front door . . . The flower garden," the paper added, "is now ablaze with color."

Freud was soon out walking in the garden, which abutted Primrose Hill, with Regent's Park in the background. Confined inside his apartment during the Nazi takeover, Freud, who was in his way a nature lover, had become starved for light and air. The first time that he walked through the small garden at the Elsworthy Road house, he threw back his head, thrust out his arms and said, "I am almost tempted to cry out, 'Heil Hitler.'"

Yet Freud's feelings were actually more complex. On the day he got to London, he sat down and wrote a letter to his friend Max Eitingon, in which he revealed something of his inner state. "The emotional climate of these days is hard to grasp," Freud said, "almost indescribable. The feeling of triumph on being liberated is too strongly mixed with sorrow, for in spite of everything I still greatly loved the prison from which I have been released. The enchantment of the new surroundings (which make one want to shout 'Heil Hitler') is blended with discontent caused by little peculiarities of the strange environment; the happy anticipations of a new life are dampened by the question: how long will a fatigued heart be able to accomplish any work?"

And yet, almost despite himself, Freud began to feel at home in England. He had first come to the country in 1875, at the age of nineteen, to visit relatives in Manchester. Two years before the visit, Freud was already developing into a committed Anglophile: to his friend, Eduard Silberstein, he wrote: "I am reading English poems, writing English letters, declaiming English verse, listening to English descriptions, and thirsting after English views." Freud was delighted by what he found in Manchester and even thought of emigrating to England. When he returned home, Freud wrote again to Silberstein, saying, "I would rather live there than here, in spite of fog and rain, drunkenness and conservatism. Many peculiarities of the English character and country which other continentals would find intolerable fit in very well with my nature." From then on, Freud venerated England and English culture; he even named one of his sons Oliver, after Oliver Cromwell, the leader of the Puritan revolution. Surely there was now still a chance that what Freud had said sixty years ago was true and that England was something like his spiritual home.

The initial greetings Freud received when he returned to England now in 1938 might have convinced him of as much. Two days after his arrival, Freud, who was never easy to surprise, was genuinely taken aback by what he encountered. "Here there is enough to write about," he said, "most of it pleasant, some very pleasant. The reception in Victoria Station and then in the newspapers of the first few days was most kind, indeed enthusiastic. We are buried in flowers. Interesting letters come: only three collectors of autographs, a painter who wants to make a portrait when I have rested, etc." There was also a four-page telegram signed by "citizens of all faiths and professions," from Cleveland, Ohio, USA, inviting Freud to come to the heartland of America and make his home there. "We shall have to answer," Freud said, "that we have already unpacked."

What struck Freud the most were the many letters from strangers who were simply writing to say how happy they were that Freud and his family had arrived safely and peacefully in England. "Really," Freud added, "as if our concerns were theirs as well." Valuable antiquities came to Freud as gifts from people he had never met, but who knew that his adored collection was still in Austria. Taxi drivers were aware of the Freuds' whereabouts and whisked Anna home; the bank manager said, "I know all about you." Letters with the address "Sigmund Freud/London" came to the door. Said Freud, "England is a blessed, a happy land, inhabited by kindly hospitable people; that at least is the impression of the first weeks." The experience was stunning to Freud, who was finally tasting the public rewards of his long labors, finally feeling the recognition that his achievement and innovation deserved. "For the first time and late in life," he declared, "I have experienced what fame means."

Was Freud not famous in Vienna? From early in his career, Freud had been the doctor that singularly open-minded members of the Viennese middle class went to see when all the respectable options failed them. He was known for his peculiar techniques—hypnotism (though only for a while); the analysis of dreams; free association; a willingness to take the parapraxes, slips of the tongue and the pen, seriously. He was understood to be eccentric, brilliant, and perhaps a little dangerous. The unrelenting Karl Kraus sustained a constant attack on Freud and his doctrines: "Psychoanalysis," he sneered, "is the disease of which it purports to be the cure." That meant, among other things, that Freud's insistence on the determining power of childhood, trauma, and the past could become an obsession for a given individual, who, having encountered Freud's theories, would begin to think of nothing else. How to cure such an obsession? Well, only Sigmund Freud could begin to do that. In the early phase of his career, Freud had been infamous among many in Vienna; later he had been notorious. But even as his renown expanded across the world, Freud never tasted the day-to-day pleasures of fame, at least until he arrived in England.

Here in England he was recognized in the street (on the odd occasion he went outside); he was praised in the newspapers; he was the object of warm solicitude on the part of people he had never met (including, from afar, the leading citizens of Cleveland, Ohio). So this is what it felt like to be famous! This was what Goethe enjoyed and, closer to the present, what Freud's friend Einstein had the chance to savor every day. Freud, clearly, was taken by surprise, not only by his ascension to fame and goodwill, but also by how much he liked it.

Yet on some level, Freud probably felt that what he was experiencing was a form of "intoxication." After all, he was the one who had no use for alcohol, no use for religion, no use, during the great part of his life, for romantic love—the over-estimation of the object, as he liked to call it. Freud endorsed the life of spiritual sobriety and of inner and outer struggle. The psyche was a divided entity: to allow that division to be quelled for a protracted period was a formula for delusion and maybe disaster. He had spent his entire life in conflict with what he thought of as the "social superego." He'd always said the painful, nonpolitic thing: he had announced to the world that children are sexually hypercharged; he had insisted that we were inhabited by a strange impersonal force that determined our destinies in ways that most of us can barely understand; he had told people—maybe this was the most insulting thing of all—that they did not know why their own jokes were funny. All his life he had struggled against the external forces of social disapproval, which, his theory of the superego insisted, had an internal bearing as well. The over-I is, among other things, a precipitate of social strictures, an internalization of the frequently unwritten laws the collective will works to impose. We are society: society lives within us and is made strong by our own vital energies. So he who would struggle against society must struggle against a part of himself. The person willing to contend against the social norm must, accordingly, be ready to feel what amount to self-inflicted wounds.

Freud savored opposition: he had said that he always needed a foe to strive against as well as a staunch ally to support him. He had said that being a Jew, with the long history of persecution to look back on, was excellent preparation for doing his intellectual work in the world. "Nor is it perhaps entirely a matter of chance that the first advocate of psychoanalysis was a Jew," he said. "To profess belief in this new theory called for a certain degree of readiness to accept a situation of solitary opposition—a situation with which no one is more familiar than a Jew." But savor struggle as he might—not for nothing was Freud an admirer of Milton's Satan, the arch-rebel—struggle with the social norm was always going to be a source of anxiety. Almost as much as he loved opposition, Freud loved success, recognition, and all the secure trappings of bourgeois life.

Freud presumably understood that most of the people casually praising him here in England had not read a complete volume of his and that if they had, and could understand it, their reactions would range from incredulity to outrage. Maybe he was getting mildly inebriated, and maybe more than that, from what he—no democrat, no egalitarian—would have recognized as an especially cheap vintage, the praise of the newspaper-reading public. Freud, late in life, now faced a dilemma: Should he continue to be benignly gracious, enjoy his standing, and go gently? Or should he be Freud, the exuberant troublemaker, down to the end?

Freud had on his desk at 39 Elsworthy Road the third chapter of his Moses book, the chapter that would be by far the most incendiary. When it was completed—if it was—and bound together with the first two chapters, the book would create, if not a firestorm (there was too much happening on the larger stage of the world for that), then at the very least real controversy and surely some antipathy too. When Freud had been working on the book in Vienna, he understood that its publication would cause him problems: it was, he wrote, "bound to be something fundamentally new and shattering to the uninitiated. Concern for these uninitiated compels me to keep the completed essay secret."

Even in England the Moses book would more than likely bring an end to the acceptance and affection that Freud was enjoying. (Perhaps the only time in his life when he had encountered a comparable feeling of acceptance was in 1909, when he came to America and experienced what he called the "incredible daydream." But Freud had only contempt for the United States; for England, the country that now welcomed him, he felt something like adulation: in this love affair the affection flowed both ways.) Freud, sick as he was, old as he was, a refugee, with all the vulnerabilities of the newcomer in an adopted country, had to decide if he would dare to go forward. "I don't anticipate a friendly reception from the scientific critics," Freud said. "Jewry will be very offended." The two chapters of the Moses book that Freud had already published were in German and in a rather obscure journal, *Imago*. Yet there were already people who had read them and had their worried intimations about the third. Soon they began to bring pressure on Freud.

It is worth noting that happiness—if that is what Freud was experiencing in London—was something that Freudian thinking has very little commerce with. When it comes to describing human beings at their best, Freud has little to say. He can touch on genius when he describes failed or failing erotic love, accounts for jealousy, or maps the subtle dynamics of self-subversion. He can explain why one person is a miser, another is a hypochondriac, a third an inveterate ingrate. He can describe the dynamics of tyranny in striking ways. When adults act like dismaying children, Freud, better perhaps than anyone, illuminates the scene.

But of course if Freud is right, the human capacity for regression is always present. The hunger for Hitler, or someone like him, never really goes away. The urge to be cruel, be destructive, be brutal, is perpetually there. By describing people at their worst, one is nonetheless getting close to something like their essence. Some people have seen Freud as a reductionist; perhaps it is better to see him as someone with brilliant insights into human beings when they are at their most reduced.

In Freud's descriptions of humanity at its worst, he barely takes into account history, or economics, or the specific qualities of a given culture. He has no interest in thinking about how various external pressures—the loss of a horrible war, an unfair treaty, alternating periods of inflation and depression—could help bring on the tyranny he describes in *Group Psychology*. Freud is not at all interested in pondering the relations between perceived cultural chaos and the onset of the kind of fundamentalist religion he describes in *Future of an Illusion*.

Freud once remarked that the objective of psychoanalysis was to transform hysterical misery into common, everyday unhappiness. In saying so, he exhibited not only his personal temperament, but also his thinking's bandwidth. Freud is a superb student of misery and unhappiness, but about what makes life worth living, he has surprisingly little to say. Freud cannot contribute much to understanding what makes a happy marriage or a flourishing family life. He cannot tell where genuinely consequential art comes from: he can offer a superb analysis of Hamlet the character, but not of *Hamlet* the play. Hamlet the character he can treat like a patient of his, though a singularly complex one; the play itself, in its freshness and power, passes beyond his terms of analysis. Similarly, he cannot explain how an individual moves past narcissism or the will to personal power, and lives for the good of others or for the good of humanity as a whole.

This is true because for Freud all human behavior is defined by its origins in childhood. The childhood past (like the primitive past, as Freud sees it) is inevitably tormented; Freud's child always wants what he cannot have and has what he does not want. To Freud, the present is fundamentally a repetition of what has come before: in fact there is, strictly speaking, no pure present, no "now," in the thought of Sigmund Freud.

On the matter of unhappiness, Freud's work suggests that we might reverse Tolstoy's famous observation. From the Freudian perspective, it is all the unhappy families that are more or less alike. They repeat and repeat the old patterns of frustrated desire and mysterious aggression. In them the dynamics of the Oedipal complex are in full and constant play: the past is all and the present virtually nonexistent. The Dutch psychoanalyst, J. H. van den Berg evokes this limit to Freud's thinking when he observes that "the theory of repression . . . is closely related to the thesis that there is a sense in everything, which in turn implies that everything is past and there is nothing new." Freud's thought cannot encompass something new, something not directly and definingly related to the repressed past. He could never really explain how people broke the mold—how they did unpredictable, productive things. Freud, one might say, had no theory that could begin to explain how someone as original and bold as Sigmund Freud ever existed.

Perhaps one of the reasons Freud distrusted democracy so much is that if he had admitted its promise, he would also have had to admit that human beings could develop a fresh, effective way of governing themselves, which swerved away from the old familial patterns of domination (father over all). Freud intended to write a paper on the dynamics of sublimation—that is, on the way that instinctual energies stop sustaining old patterns and move on to invest the creation of fresh achievements in commerce, art, and science—but he never managed to do it. Freud can account for our behavior but not our acts, our sorrow but not our happiness.

Freud in London now, in 1938, feeling better than he had in a long time, was facing a perplexing condition. Struggle and strife he was abundantly accustomed to; he knew all the dynamics (and the pleasures) of conflict. And he believed that he knew all the vicissitudes of intoxication as well. But was this feeling of pleasure at arriving in a free nation perhaps something else: might it be that strange, elusive thing called happiness?

*　　*　　*

On Friday, June 10, Freud went off to visit his chow, Lün, who had been taken from Dover, where the Freud party landed, off to a quarantine kennel at Ladbroke Grove. The trip garnered some media attention: "Nothing could have kept the great scientist away from his dog friend," Michael Molnar quotes an Australian sports newspaper, the *Referee*, as saying. The paper went on to cite the kennel's director, who averred, " 'I have never seen such happiness and understanding in an animal's eyes. . . . [Freud] played with her, talked to her, using all sorts of little terms of endearment, for fully an hour. And, though the journey is long for a man of his years, he said that he was resolute about coming to see Lün as often as he can.' " Here and elsewhere around him in his new home, Freud could find a new image for himself, a not-an-entirely-disagreeable one: that of the mellow, sweet-natured magus, benignly savoring ripe old age.

The next day, Freud received a visit from Abraham Shalom Yahuda, a Jewish Bible scholar who also lived on Elsworthy Road. Yahuda is the first visitor to the new house in England whose arrival Freud notes in his diary, though he does misspell the scholar's name as *Jahuda*, a sign perhaps of Freud's overall feelings about the visit. Yahuda came to meet his distinguished neighbor, to welcome him to England and to pay due respects, but he had another purpose as well. He wanted to entreat Freud not to publish the Moses book. The Jews, Yahuda said, were already facing enough tribulations in the world, which was of course something that Freud, the refugee from Hitler's Austria, knew as well as anyone. Why should Freud want to add to the Jews' many woes by publishing what was bound to be an inflammatory—perhaps even an anti-Semitic—book? Yahuda, it seems, was aware that Freud was going to go so far as to question Moses's identity as a Jew.

Yahuda was not the only one who begged Freud to drop the Moses project. The same month, Freud wrote to Arnold Zweig about receiving a letter "from a young American Jew imploring me not to deprive our poor unhappy people of the only consolation remaining to them in their misery." Then Freud asked, a bit too ingenuously, "Is it really credible that my dry essay, even were it to reach him, should disturb the belief of a single believer conditioned by heredity and upbringing?" On June 21, Freud, so far undaunted by opposition, internal or external, went back to work on the Moses book, trying to mold the refractory third essay into shape.

Freud had already written forcefully against religion in the 1927 volume *Future of an Illusion*. There he describes Western faith as nostalgically and oppressively patriarchal. Human beings long for the father, he says; more precisely, they long for the childhood father's return. At one time, Freud says, almost all of us lived in total security, or at least in the illusion of total security. For in early life, the father offers the child what seems to be complete protection and also a clear, unassailable sense of right and wrong. As people grow, they inevitably lose faith in their individual parents, who reveal themselves as flawed, inadequate, lacking in judgment, and anything but omnipotent. They are not the perfect beings that children, early on, take them to be. Yet as Freud insists throughout his work—the idea is at the core of his thinking—people will never voluntarily leave what they have once felt to be a fully satisfying emotional situation. The id, once it has committed itself to a given object or idea and found that commitment to be fulfilling, resists letting go with all its might. A patriot loves his country to the death, right or wrong; a woman continues to adore the cheating husband who once gave her joy; the father never stops mourning his departed child. When reality deprives us of something we love, our first impulse, and often our last, is to reconstitute it through fantasy. There are few more satisfying situations, Freud says, than the feeling that we are protected and watched over by an all-loving superior being, who knows with certainty the distinction between right and wrong, true and false. When our judgment shows that no such figure actually exists, the psyche rebels and re-creates a Supreme Being in conformity with its wishes. This occurs in religion and also, of course, in politics. So the father of merely mortal nature is reconfigured and reborn as the immortal sky god and as the omnipotent leader.

Freud asserts that human beings combat their feelings of helplessness in a hostile world by concocting a collective supreme fiction: "When the growing individual finds that he is destined to remain a child for ever, that he can never do without protection against strange superior powers, he lends those powers the features belonging to the figure of his father; he creates for himself the gods whom he dreads, whom he seeks to propitiate, and whom he nevertheless entrusts with his own protection. Thus his longing for a father is a motive identical with his need for protection against the consequences of his human weakness."

Like the dictator, the patriarchal god is an answer to the crisis of the superego. The superego, at its worst, is unconscious, overly demanding, and cruel, often to the point of sadism. It punishes us, Freud insists in *Civilization and Its Discontents*, not only for the transgressions we commit, but also for those that we merely conceive of committing: it disciplines not only the act, but also the desire. The external superego, the patriarchal sky god, can be cruel and demanding as well, but he has also left mankind his commandments. Through his scriptures and his prophecy, people understand what placates him, or perhaps even what wins his favor. Like the dictator, the sky god introduces clarity into situations that are disturbingly over-complicated. Now we know what is just and what is not; now we know how to conduct ourselves so as to assure prosperity on this earth and salvation in the next. "Thus," says Freud in *Future of an Illusion*, "the benevolent rule of a divine Providence allays our fear of the dangers of life; the establishment of a moral world-order ensures the fulfillment of the demands of justice, which have so often remained unfulfilled in human civilization; and the prolongation of human existence in a future life provides the local and temporal framework in which these wish-fulfillments shall take place." Human beings, Freud suggests, wish perhaps more than anything else to find the Truth, the one right way to live in the world, and then to organize their lives around it. One of Freud's major hypotheses in the last phase of his work is that people would usually rather have Truth through union with what is greater than themselves than have pleasure that they can enjoy for its own sake, moment to moment and day to day. It often feels better to have absolute meaning in life than it does to have stimulation, variety, complexity—a world rich and marvelous but not entirely explicable. The cost of a relatively open-ended existence can be fierce anxiety—anxiety most people are desperate to discharge as expeditiously as possible. Recall Hitler's telling lines: "The masses love a commander more than a petitioner and feel inwardly more satisfied by a doctrine, tolerating no other beside itself, than by the granting of liberalistic freedom with which, as a rule, they can do little, and are prone to feel that they have been abandoned."

Freud suggests that the qualities that culture has associated with women—love, nurture, care—are not ultimately the qualities that human beings want to spend their lives pursuing and possessing. What we seem to desire most, men and women both, is to get ourselves into stabilizing contact with power and authority. We want to find those things, subordinate ourselves to them, and to do so we will, if necessary, forego love and all the other intimate human satisfactions. In his late writings, Freud stops thinking so much about the Oedipal desire of the mother, which he comes to feel that individuals may be able to surmount in time, and begins thinking more about the human hunger for patriarchs, about the need for kings.

When Freud published *Future of an Illusion* in 1927, many Anglo-European intellectuals were declaring that religion was gradually withering away. Even in the mid-nineteenth century, writers like Matthew Arnold were worried about the world that would come into being when humanity had done the seemingly inevitable and ended its commitment to transcendental faith. The world might then become a place where, in the well-known line, "ignorant armies clash by night." Arnold and others like him expended considerable intellectual effort trying to figure out what to do when the day came and faith was fully extinguished. This is something that even Nietzsche—who was not terribly prone to handwringing— worries about, perhaps most famously in his passage on the death of God in *The Gay Science.* "'How shall we comfort ourselves, the murderers of all murderers?'" asks Nietzsche's madman, who in this case is probably close to being identical with Nietzsche himself. "'What was holiest and mightiest of all that the world has yet owned has bled to death under our knives: who will wipe this blood off us? What water is there for us to clean ourselves? What festivals of atonement, what sacred games shall we have to invent? Is not the greatness of this deed too great for us?'" Then comes the ultimate Nietzschean question: "'Must we ourselves not become gods simply to appear worthy of it?'" Karl Marx, Thomas Carlyle, Jeremy Bentham, John Stuart Mill, Ernest Renan, Charles Darwin, John Ruskin, Alfred Lord Tennyson—each in his way registered a sense that in his generation or the next, religion would die away.

Though there is a superficial optimism in *Future of an Illusion* about the birth of a comprehensive atheism, the main thrust of Freud's thinking about religion and the addiction to the patriarch brings no such hope. To Freud, the essence of Western religion—and he would surely include Islam in the indictment as well—is fundamentalism. People yearn to believe in a monolithic, all-seeing and all-knowing deity who controls life on earth and throughout the cosmos. Fundamentalism is at the heart of religion because it represents the most direct and intense recapitulation of the early state of things where the father and his powers were all. (The novelist Salman Rushdie avers that people have "a God-shaped hole" within them and Freud would surely agree.) All father religions, Freud indicates, have fundamentalism at their core, so that the believer, however nuanced or humane his belief may appear, can always be pulled as if by gravitational force back to unquestioning commitment to the father and his unerring word.

Accordingly, Freud does not go out of his way in *Future of an Illusion* to commend the less overtly patriarchal faiths. Fundamentalism is like tyranny—and like love and liquor—an intoxicant, and the only way to overcome fundamentalism is to cut off faith completely. Freud's answer to authoritarian religion is not personal religious experience, outside of institutional structures, which William James commends in *Varieties of Religious Experience*, nor is it that vague amalgam that, since Freud's time, has come to be called spirituality. Freud's recommendation is complete withdrawal from the drug, and that withdrawal takes the form of a militant atheism. Belief in no god is Freud's answer to what he takes to be the infantilizing force of faith. And once god is gone, the individual will do well to beware of god substitutes, which come in myriad forms, from leaders to social causes to patriotic dogmas to fervent commitments to this ruling idea or that. Sometimes, of course, atheists are among the most overbearingly religious people in the world, for they have displaced their will to believe onto some other absolute—or, they have made their atheism itself into something like an evangelical faith.

Because human beings need leaders to organize their collective lives, Freud believes that they should seek out humane,
relatively un-self-interested people who have done something to
conquer their own narcissism and their will to power. Always,
though, there will be a risk of tyranny, for that is, after all, what
human beings most want. The American diplomat and writer
George Kennan seems to feel that he is offering a bracing truth
when he says that, "The fact of the matter is that there is a little
bit of the totalitarian buried somewhere, way down deep, in
each and every one of us." Were Freud to hear this, he would
probably laugh aloud. To Freud, Sylvia Plath is closer to the
truth: "Every woman adores a Fascist," she famously declared in
"Daddy": from Freud's perspective, every man does too.

For his conviction about the allure of the patriarch, Freud
was not without evidence, nor has evidence been lacking for it
in the years after his death. Hitler and Mussolini may have
fallen, but there were also Stalin and Mao and Franco, and all
the dictators large and small who have lorded it over often-
worshipful masses in Africa and Asia, Latin America and Eastern
Europe. Force has helped establish and consolidate these
leaders, it's true, but often the adulation of the tyrannized
for their tyrants has been of no little consequence either. Nor
has religion become more comprehensively enlightened over
time. In the twenty-first century a stranglingly intolerant version of faith is abroad not only throughout the Islamic world,
but in the United States of America. Fundamentalist faiths have
a number of identifying dimensions: belief in the absolute and
unambiguous truth of this or that scripture; a sense of embattled
righteousness; rule by males and a concomitant repression of

women; pursuit of holy struggle and perhaps, in time, of holy war; a sense of pervasive crisis in the world; a demand for unquestioning obedience. But most saliently, for Freud, there is the presence of the patriarchal god, looking down on his worshippers, issuing his harsh but luminous commands, and blessing his chosen ones above all others.

It is hard to escape the view that when people subordinate themselves to cruel dictatorships and tyrannical deities, they are satisfying needs that are, among other things, psychological, infantile. They are creating sound, solid identities for themselves, rather than exploring human possibility. Freud pointed to the twofold horror of what one might call the patriarchal complex, tyrannical governments and tyrannical religions, and began to explain why they will probably be with us forever. This is true despite the fact that such governments and religions are palpably contrary to collective interests, and even frequently to the interests of the dictators and hysterical preachers themselves. Their fate is often epitomized by Benito Mussolini, who ended amply perforated with bullets and strung up in the public square in Milan.

But Freud didn't merely intend to repeat himself in the Moses book: he had, he believed, something new to say. He wanted to understand the character of Moses, a figure he had admired through his life; he wanted to get to the bottom of what made the Jews the people that they were; he wanted to arrive at a psychoanalytical explanation for anti-Semitism. More than that, the book he was writing would be an indirect autobiography and a meditation on what psychoanalysis was and what it might become. But Freud had been working on the book now for at least four years and had declared it finished more than once, only to return to it for more development. The Moses book, he wrote to Ernest Jones, "plagues me like a 'ghost not laid.' I wonder if I shall still manage to pull together this third part, despite all the external and internal difficulties. For the time being, I cannot believe it. But *quien sabe?*"

On June 23, two days after taking up work on the Moses book again, Freud got a taste of what was perhaps the most flattering elixir that England could dispense. Three secretaries of the Royal Society, Sir Albert Seward, Professor A. V. Hill, and Griffith Davies, came to visit Freud at home to ask him to sign the society's charter book. In general, only the king, an honorary member of the society, actually had the book brought to him to sign; all others had to make their way to the society for it. But Freud, because he was unwell and could not readily travel to Burlington House, had the book brought to him. (Two weeks before, Freud had managed to go out and journey to see his dog, Lün, at the quarantine kennel, but the Royal Society couldn't seem to elicit the same commitment from Freud as his beloved chow.) Freud signed his name beneath that of Isaac Newton, and also of Charles Darwin, one of the figures Freud most admired and whose work he saw as a prelude to his own. For years he had been signing only his last name to letters and documents: Freud. But in England, signing with the last name only was the prerogative of a lord, so Freud, for what may have been the first time in forty years, was compelled to sign his whole name.

Surely the Royal Society honor was official public testimony that Sigmund Freud was what he had always, at least in some part of his spirit, aspired to be and feared he was not, a scientist. In fact, Freud was never entirely sure how to describe his work. His most passionate, overt hope was that psychoanalysis was in fact scientific. He had started out as an empirical researcher, after all, working on, among other things, the structure of the medulla oblongata, the hindmost section of the brain, which he once described as a "very beautiful object." As speculative as his work became—in time he would offer theories of the compulsion to repeat, the Death Drive, and the titanic strife between what he called Eros and Thanatos—Freud nonetheless held on to the hope that, in time, biological data would arise to confirm all his hypotheses.

At other times, Freud took a different view: he said that the poets were there before him; they were the first true students of the unconscious. The difference between Freud's knowledge and the poets' was simply that the poets had proceeded by intuition, whereas Freud managed to build a systematic account. Freud referred to his theory of the drives, which he was constantly reformulating, as "our mythology." He called himself a "conquistador" because of his swashbuckling intellectual ambitions; and he confessed that he always aspired to be a philosophe, a thinker in the mode of Voltaire, who took up all of the major questions, from the cosmic to the intensely private, and did so with freewheeling and spontaneous, if also highly cultivated, intelligence.

Yet Freud understood that a scientific identity, especially in the first half of the twentieth century, when the prestige of science was compounding, would give him a larger share of cultural authority. It would mean that more people would listen to him and take him seriously. Freud feared, and rightly, that psychoanalysis was perpetually in danger of being dismissed as the palmistry or phrenology of its day. To be known as a scientist would help to solidify the new standing that Freud had achieved on his arrival in London. Signing the Royal Society book made Freud look more like what he had always wanted, or half wanted, to be: a man of science, who opened up the secrets of life.

And yet, Freud knew that the new book was not going to be science. It would speculate, supported by thin enough evidence, that Moses was not a Jew but an Egyptian; that monotheism was an Egyptian innovation, brought to the Jews by Moses; and that the Jews eventually murdered Moses for his pains. To publish such a book would surely be to undermine the gift that the magi of the Royal Society had brought to Freud, inclusion in the coterie of serious and estimable men, men of science. Why not do the expedient thing? Why not simply let society tell you who and what you are, especially when its verdict flatters long-maintained wishes—for success, for status, and of course, in a certain sense, for love—that have been frustrated for a long time?

Perhaps it would have been best if Freud were willing to think of his writing as something like "wisdom literature." After Freud's death and before it, many critics of his work have demonstrated that it does not stand up to the strict requirements of science: the findings he offers are not quantifiable, not repeatable, not falsifiable. These critics have actually done Freud a service. They have released him from a standard that he cannot meet and helped to redefine his work in ways that will in time allow its true value to emerge. Freud may have covered his office with pictures of the scientists, or aspirants to science, whom he most admired, men like Charcot and Helmholtz. But his real intellectual predecessors were, most directly, Schopenhauer and Nietzsche, philosophers who were both speculative and practical. (Freud once said that he had not read much of Nietzsche, virtually all of whose books he nonetheless owned, because he was afraid that in Nietzsche's work he would find too many of the truths of psychoanalysis anticipated.) Freud provides a way of looking at experience that—like Samuel Johnson's way, or Montaigne's or Emerson's—can be proved or disproved not by scientific standards, but by individuals deploying his ideas and honestly chronicling the gains and losses that follow. No one has ever lost sleep wondering if Montaigne is a scientist, nor should anyone do so about Freud. Philip Rieff and, later, Adam Phillips have led the way in understanding Freud as a possible guide to life, a post-religious thinker whose concepts have a practical use, or as William James would say, a cash value, if they have any value at all.

But Freud never took this path, never identified himself with Nietzsche and Schopenhauer: Freud thought that the only way he could genuinely succeed was as a scientist. He had been preoccupied with the matter of success on the grand scale from early in his life. Freud frequently recalled that when he was a child, a Gypsy told his mother that he would accomplish great things and that his mother had readily believed it. She liked to call her son "my golden Siggy" and gave him every chance to advance himself in the world. He had his own room in a small, very crowded house and all were compelled to keep quiet while he did his work; his sister Anna recalls having to stop her piano playing so that Freud could concentrate. Freud's father loved and admired his son, but his mother believed in him with an incandescent faith. Later in life, Freud would say that the most important condition for a man's success in life was the unqualified love and confidence of his mother, and this he enjoyed.

In *The Interpretation of Dreams*, Freud recalls a particular incident that he forever after associated with his desire to succeed. "When I was seven or eight years old," he says, "there is [a] domestic scene which I can remember very clearly. One evening before going to sleep I disregarded the rules which modesty lays down and obeyed the calls of nature in my parents' bedroom while they were present. In the course of his reprimand, my father let fall the words, 'The boy will come to nothing.'" Freud says that this must have been a "frightful blow," because when in later life he thought of the scene, he always began to enumerate his achievements and successes, as if to say to his father: "You see, I have come to something." Forever after, Freud would associate urinating in public or involuntarily losing control of one's bladder with strong ambition. "Look at me!" the perpetrator wants to say. Though what he's done is hardly commendable, he still wants attention so badly that he'll suffer embarrassment to get it. Perhaps later he'll find more apt ways to draw the crowd's gaze, but for now this is what's in his repertoire.

Freud was no longer a child and no longer needed to soak himself in front of others to get the attention he wanted. He had earned what he desired so much from childhood through hard work and daring. Freud remarked once that getting rich doesn't make people happy because happiness only comes from the fulfillment of childhood wishes. It may be that no three-year-old wishes for a strong and amply diversified portfolio, but surely a young child can hunger after fame. Now the Royal Society testified to Sigmund Freud's standing. It must have been tempting to imagine how he could stand back, forget about the Moses project for a while, and enjoy what he had earned.

But Freud had been intrigued by Moses for quite some time. In 1914, the year that Freud's work underwent a major change, and his fascination with the issue of authority began to crystallize, Freud published his anonymous article about Michelangelo's statue of the prophet. Freud had seen it in the church of Saint Peter in Chains in Rome and become transfixed. "I stood in the church in front of the statue," he wrote, "studying it, measuring it, and drawing it." (Freud was a surprisingly good draftsman.) The brief essay, which came out in *Imago*, was, according to Freud, an attempt to figure out why the statue had the allure for him that it did. Freud says that when he cannot explain how a work of art achieves its effect, he cannot obtain any real pleasure from it. "Some rationalistic, or perhaps analytic, turn of mind in me rebels against being moved by a thing without knowing why I am thus affected and what it is that affects me."

The sculpture depicts the prophet clasping tightly on to the Ten Commandments, which he has just brought down from Mount Sinai. Freud is curious about what Moses is actually doing with the tablets of the law. Conventional interpretation has it that he is about to hurl them down at the Israelites who are dancing around the golden calf. But Freud believes that Michelangelo had something much different in mind. For, Freud says, the prophet, as he's depicted, has not given in to anything like full-fledged anger. He isn't about to visit holy wrath on the wayward people. Rather, Michelangelo's Moses is a divided being: he is angry, yes, but he is also in the process of containing the emotion. "In his first transport of fury," Freud says, "Moses desired to act, to spring up and take revenge and forget the Tables; but he has overcome the temptation and he will now remain seated and still, in his frozen wrath and in his pain mingled with contempt. Nor will he throw away the Tables so that they will break on the stones." Freud's Moses has contained his anger, kept his passion in check.

Freud believes that the sculptor swerved away from the biblical text to assert that Moses, enraged though he was about the Israelites' transgression, nonetheless manages to control himself. He is, to use Freud's idiom, sublimating his anger rather than giving in to it, and it is, presumably, from his ability to sublimate that he gains his authority as a leader. Michelangelo, Freud says, "has added something new and more than human to the figure of Moses; so that the giant frame with its tremendous physical power becomes only a concrete expression of the highest mental achievement that is possible in a man, that of struggling successfully against an inward passion for the sake of a cause to which he has devoted himself."

The authority Moses achieves in his self-division is unconventional, from the perspective of Freud's later work, in that, in general, authority comes from appearing to be completely at one with oneself. The leader knows at all times what he thinks about all things, and he is always right. His presence is constantly, as Freud says in *Group Psychology*, masterful and self-assured. But in Moses, Freud believes that he is confronting someone who is certainly a leader but who nonetheless is able to dramatize his self-division. Moses—or at least Moses as Freud believes the sculptor sees him—is manifestly candid about the state of his interior life. Presumably his standing as a leader comes from that honesty. He is able to reflect the authentic state of his followers' psyches, for they too (like all of us) are prone to be divided, yet they nonetheless accept him as an authority.

It's possible that Freud is suggesting that this power of dramatic sublimation is characteristically Jewish. And he may also be suggesting that he himself, by virtue of his capacity to discern the feat of sublimation that Moses enacts, may embody this presumably rare power—and so be able to lead humanely. "Moses," Freud will say at the very end of his life, "is flesh of sublimation," and in this enigmatic remark he concentrates much of what makes the prophet so fascinating to him.

In London now, Freud continues to work. Quite sick, not fully rested from his journey, he sits in his unfamiliar study on Elsworthy Road and speculates about Moses. His beloved collection is still in Vienna under the control of the Nazis and might never return. On his desk he has a few terra-cottas given to him by the princess when he stopped in Paris on the way to England; in the midst of them is posed his treasured figure of Athena, the warrior intellect. He has few books at his disposal because his library remains under Gestapo control. Lün, who usually sits by him while he writes, purring gruffly and diffusing her doggy smell, which to Freud is more than agreeable, is still quarantined at the kennel. He is officially forbidden cigars, but it's hard to imagine that he doesn't enjoy one from time to time, since they are, after all, the food of thought. Against no little resistance, Sigmund Freud keeps going.

In mid-July, Freud received a visit from a longtime admirer, the Spanish surrealist painter Salvador Dalí. Dalí—handsome, loquacious, self-promoting—had for many years wanted to meet Freud, whom he thought of as one of the major influences on his paintings and on the surrealist movement. In his autobiography, *The Secret Life of Salvador Dalí*, Dalí recalls his early attempts to meet with the great man. "My three voyages to Vienna," he says, "were exactly like three drops of water which lacked the reflections to make them glitter. On each of these voyages I did exactly the same things: in the morning I went to see the Vermeer in the Czernin Collection, and in the afternoon I did *not* go to visit Freud because I invariably learned that he was out of town for reasons of health." Dalí recalls instead spending his afternoons walking haphazardly through the streets of Vienna, eating chocolate tarts, which, he claims, possessed a bitterness accentuated by the meeting that never took place. "In the evening," he recalls, "I held long and exhaustive imaginary conversations with Freud; he came home with me once and stayed all night clinging to the curtains of my room in the Hotel Sacher."

A few years after his last failed attempt to see Freud, Dalí was sitting in a restaurant in France, eating a dish of snails and talking with his companions about Marie Bonaparte's recently published book on Edgar Allan Poe. All of a sudden, Dalí says, he saw a picture of none other than Sigmund Freud on the cover of a newspaper and learned that Freud had escaped from Austria and just arrived in Paris. "We had not yet recovered from this news," Dalí says, "when I uttered a loud cry. I had just that instant discovered the morphological secret of Freud! Freud's cranium is a snail! His brain is in the form of a spiral—to be extracted with a needle!"

On July 19, a little more than a month after Freud got to London, Dalí, in company with Freud's friend Stefan Zweig, made his way to Elsworthy Road, where he finally had the chance to meet the Professor. As he approached the house, the artist encountered something arresting. "I saw a bicycle leaning against the wall, and on the saddle, attached by a string, was a red rubber hot-water bottle which looked full of water, and on the back of the hot-water bottle walked a snail!"

Dalí had high expectations for the meeting, though it's not entirely clear what those expectations were. Perhaps Dalí aspired to be anointed as Freud's first authentic visual disciple, or maybe—Dalí was nothing if not confident—Freud's coeval. Just as Freud had described the unconscious in detail, so perhaps Dalí—with his paintings of melting clocks and inner deserts and gaudily misshapen human forms—aspired to render that unconscious, to make its productions visible. Perhaps Freud would bless his work and tell him that he had gotten things exactly right. If Dalí did have such expectations, he did not know much about the character of Sigmund Freud.

For the entire time they sat in Freud's study, Freud hardly said a word. ("We devoured each other with our eyes," Dalí asserted.) Freud had just suffered another attack of temporary deafness brought on by an infection, but in all probability, Dalí knew nothing of this. To Dalí, Freud was simply a great stone face. At one point in the visit, a frustrated Dalí tried to draw Freud's interest to his article on the subject of paranoia. "I explained that it was not a surrealist diversion, but was really an ambitiously scientific article, and I repeated the title, pointing to it at the same time with my finger. Before his imperturbable indifference, my voice became involuntarily sharper and more insistent. Then, continuing to stare at me with a fixity in which his whole being seemed to converge, Freud exclaimed, addressing Stefan Zweig, 'I have never seen a more complete example of a Spaniard. What a fanatic!' "

But there was worse. The subject of surrealism came up and Freud informed Dalí, "In classic paintings I look for the sub-conscious—in a surrealist painting for the conscious." This, presumably, was Freud's way of saying that Dalí's apparently spontaneous dreamscapes were overly intellectual, schematic, mere illustrations of ideas—and Sigmund Freud's ideas at that. The effect was not lost on the painter. "This was the pro-nouncement," says Dalí, "of a death sentence on surrealism."

Freud's relationship to artists and to art was always, to say the least, fraught. In the essay he called "Creative Writers and Day-

Dreaming," he demeaned literary art as wishful fantasy. It allowed people to immerse themselves in pleasing delusions that were akin to their own daydreams, but more graphically presented and more fully elaborated. Through literary fantasy, the wimp becomes the gunfighter; the stay-at-home transforms himself into the world voyager. Freud's archetypal reader is not unlike the one Philip Larkin describes in his "Study of Reading Habits": he deals out justice to villains twice his size; as to women, he "clubbed" them with sex, and broke them up "like meringues." "The creative writer," Freud says in the essay, "does the same as the child at play. He creates a world of phantasy which he takes very seriously—that is, which he invests with large amounts of emotion—while separating it sharply from reality." There is, Freud argues, only one consequential differences between fantasy and creative writing and that is form. "The writer," says Freud, "softens the character of his egoistic daydream by altering and disguising it, and he bribes us by the purely formal—that is, aesthetic—yield of pleasure which he offers us in the presentation of his phantasies." Art, from this point of view, is guilt-free fantasia, egoistic dreaming that the reader can savor because of the apparent distancing that form provides. Form makes daydreaming palatable to the over-I, or so says Freud in his best known essay on the matter.

But at other moments, Freud is willing to confess that the artists are the ones who can achieve stunning insight, and do so in a flash without the hard labor that the prosaic investigator, the psychoanalyst, must invest. Even then, what the poet knows, he knows in a nonsystematic, unself-conscious way: he cannot organize and make coherently available what it is he feels. If Freud was putting on a too-somber face in front of Dalí, he might have been expressing his own anxieties about the work he was preparing to bring into the world. Freud was compelled now to see himself at least from time to time as something of an artist. One of the early working titles for the Moses book had been "Moses, a Historical Novel."

Dalí and the Royal Society, art and science—those were the borders between which Freud's work unfolded. He would love to be a scientist, so as to assume science's abundant cultural authority; but he never wanted to be constrained by the limits of empirical thinking. (Here, as elsewhere, Freud was as rebellious as he was conventional.) Freud wanted to speculate; he wanted free play for his mind. Art, too, drew Freud: he adored literature and sculpture, and wasn't immune to painting. (For music, he did not care all that much.) But art, however great, could never command the level of respect, and more important, of belief, that Freud thought psychoanalysis deserved. Part of what makes Freud's work so rich is that he was unwilling to commit himself to either side of the art/science divide. He let his urge to be imaginative and his urge to get it all absolutely right challenge, confound, and interanimate each other. This made Freud's mental life quite strong and complex, but it didn't make things terribly easy for the likes of Salvador Dalí. To be fair, though, if Freud and the visiting members of the Royal Society had gotten down to a discussion of the scientific bases of the Oedipal complex, matters would not have unfolded so smoothly either.

*　　*　　*

On one front at least, Freud had considerable reason to be satisfied. Anna had proved herself to him by the way she acted in the last days in Vienna. She had not only stood up bravely to the Gestapo; she had managed almost all the family's affairs, dealing frequently with highly placed German and Austrian Nazis. As the Freuds' liaison to Ernest Jones and the princess, Anna showed herself to be both prudent and tough. Freud, who'd long pondered the matter of his successor, left Austria sure that Anna was the right choice. Now in England, she was continuing to prove her father's judgment to have been good.

Late in July, Anna, having gone through the difficult work of procuring an alien's travel visa, went to the Fifteenth International Psychoanalytical Congress in Paris and represented Freud admirably. Standing in for her father, as she would when he was gone, Anna read a segment from the final chapter of the Moses book. And she also stood up against the Americans on the matter of lay analysis.

The Americans aspired to make psychoanalysis a part of the medical establishment: only medical doctors, they argued, should be licensed to practice Freud's therapy. Though he was himself trained as a physician, Freud did not concur. What mattered most to him was that therapists be intelligent, cultivated, and self-aware, undergo a training analysis, and be willing to submit themselves from time to time to being analyzed again, if only briefly, by a supervisor. "It is unjust and inexpedient," Freud says in *The Question of Lay Analysis*, "to try to compel a person who wants to set someone else free from the torment of a phobia or an obsession to take the roundabout road of the medical curriculum." Freud hoped that humanists would carry forward his legacy, not scientists, and the desire reveals an important dimension of his thinking. Though Freud desperately wanted respectability for psychoanalysis, he also wanted it to work, and he believed that medical training, while desirable, wasn't a crucial ingredient for creating a successful therapist. On the matter of lay analysis, Freud was, rather surprisingly, willing to put aside his hopes for institutional success and to go with more pragmatic, intuitive views. Here as elsewhere, when it came time for Freud to choose between conformity and innovation, the results were unpredictable.

On July 17 he was able to declare in his journal that the Moses book was finished. Of course, he had proclaimed as much before. But even if it was now true, questions remained. Given all the pressure against him, it was no certainty that he would go ahead and publish the book. And if he did, it was surely an open question whether he would have it translated into English and expose his new hosts directly to his thinking. But these concerns did not seem to hold Freud back, at least for the present. He was so exhilarated that he went to work on another manuscript. This would eventually become *An Outline of Psycho-analysis*, and in it Freud would hold forth on the most central and the most controversial matters of psychoanalytical doctrine. Nowhere near as speculative and adventurous as *Moses and Monotheism*, the new work was in many ways Freud's attempt to impose orthodoxy after he was gone. (Even as he was at his most adventurous, as he was with the Moses book, Freud could always find reasons to be prudent.) Whatever the new book's contents, Freud was very pleased simply to be writing again. Creation was crucial to Freud's sense of what existence was about: when he did not write, he did not feel alive.

Freud took pleasure in visits like the one he received from Salvador Dalí, and he took a good deal more pleasure from Anna's growing confidence and capability. Yet many things continued to disturb him during the days at Elsworthy Road, while his son Ernst looked for a new home for him and Martha. Freud had left four sisters in Austria, and he was worried about them. In early August, he got news that the money he left them was now at their disposal, which did something to salve his concerns, but surely not enough. Marie Bonaparte was making efforts to help them and they had other friends besides. Yet under the circumstances, Freud knew that no one could possibly accomplish enough. Princess Bonaparte was doing what she could not only for the Freud family, but for Jews generally. She even proposed purchasing a section of southern California to be used as a Jewish homeland—and was willing to contribute richly to the cause.

Freud's health continued to deteriorate. Late in August, Max Schur saw that Freud had developed a new lesion behind the area of the last operation, "more ominous because harder to reach." Schur asked Freud's surgeon, Hans Pichler, to come to London and to consider performing surgery. Pichler left Austria and arrived in London on September 7 to have a look at his famous patient.

The cancer, which Freud sometimes called "my old friend," had been with him since 1923, when he found what he first thought was a benign growth on his jaw and palate. Freud had encountered swelling in that region of his mouth as far back as 1917, but it had all but disappeared when he began smoking a particularly fine brand of cigars and so he had barely mentioned it. The growth Freud found in 1923 was too troubling to say nothing about, or to try to cure by upgrading. In April of that year, Freud's internist, Felix Deutsch came to examine Freud. "Be prepared," Freud told him, "to see something that you won't like." Deutsch didn't like it: he recognized the lesion immediately as cancerous. But he neglected to tell Freud as much, wanting to protect him from the shocking news; rather he assured his patient that the growth was benign.

Freud sought out a surgeon, Marcus Hajek, in whom he seemed to have little confidence, to have the growth excised. During the operation things went amiss—which, given Hajek's general level of skill, was all too likely—and Freud soon ended up in a small recovery room, bleeding heavily, his only companion there a rather kindly, though mentally impaired, dwarf. Freud pulled the rope on the bell to summon help, but the bell didn't work. The dwarf, seeing Freud's distress, ran off down the corridor and got help for Freud, who otherwise might well have bled to death.

Strangely enough, in 1924, Franz Kafka, perhaps Europe's greatest living writer, also came under Hajek's care. Kafka was suffering from the tuberculosis that would soon kill him, but Hajek seems to have done little or nothing for his gifted patient. When Max Brod, Kafka's close friend and editor, tried to get

Kafka more considerate treatment, Hajek "energetically explained that he could not look upon Kafka as anyone else but the patient in room number so-and-so."

Though Freud said that Hajek's procedure had greatly improved his health, all during that summer of 1923 he continued to suffer from pain in his jaw. Freud spent the summer months in Bad Gastein and then in Lavarone, Italy, on what was supposed to be a vacation. But the pain was so intense that he had to summon Felix Deutsch again, who examined his mouth, and saw that the growth was still active and that Freud would need another procedure. On September 26, Freud wrote to Ernest Jones to say that "it has now been decided that I have to undergo a new operation, a partial resection of the upper jaw as the growth reappeared on this ground. It is promised I will be able to start work 4–5 weeks later, but you know what it all means."

This time, though, Freud found himself a superior oral surgeon, Hans Pichler, who performed the operation in two stages, on October 4 and 12. Schur describes the operations this way: "On October 4, 1923 . . . the external carotid artery was ligated and an extensive dissection of the submaxillary and jugular glands was performed to prevent a spread of the cancer. Fortunately, the enlarged glands revealed no malignancy. Only on October 12 . . . did Pichler perform the radical surgery, consisting of a resection of a major part of the right maxilla, a considerable part of the mandible, the right soft palate, and the buccal (cheek) and lingual (tongue) mucous membranes." In other words, Pichler cut out a large quotient of Freud's right upper jaw and the right side of the roof of his mouth. All this was done under local anesthetic. A few weeks later, Pichler took a biopsy, found more malignant tissue, and went to work again. Then, finally, after four operations, the cancer seemed to be gone. What was left was to fit Freud with a prosthesis that would enable him to talk, to eat, and of course to smoke.

"Then," says Ernest Jones, "began sixteen years of discomfort, distress and pain." The prosthesis, "the monster," was a huge denturelike device designed to close off the mouth from the nasal cavity. It needed to come out at frequent intervals for cleaning, but removal was no easy matter, nor was reinsertion. Freud couldn't open his mouth very far, so it could sometimes take as much as half an hour to get the prosthesis back in. In doing this, Freud had one helper and one only, and that was Anna. Anna and her father made a pact that they would always deal with "the monster," and with every other thing pertaining to Freud's health, with complete detachment, as though they were a pair of surgeons working on a case together. And this they did. But "the monster" created many hardships. For Freud to eat and to talk, it needed to fit snugly. But that caused irritation and no little pain. Sores broke out on the inside of Freud's mouth. But when he took the prosthesis out to give his aching mouth a rest, the tissue that surrounded it shrunk and sometimes made reinsertion impossible. Then "the monster" had to be modified.

The prosthesis distorted Freud's speech, making it both nasal and thick. Arthur Koestler, who visited Freud in London, recalls him speaking with his lips stretched very tight and the corners of his mouth pushed out, "rather in the manner of children imitating the speech of their toothless elders in cruel mockery."

Eating also became very difficult and Freud almost never did so with others around him. The damage done to Freud's eustachian tubes by the cancer and by the operations impaired his hearing, until he became completely deaf on the right side. This was the side he had used to listen to his patients as they lay down, so he had to install himself on the other end of the couch and listen to them with his left ear.

What Freud would not do was to give up smoking. The cigars irritated his mouth, or what was left of it, so over the following years, Freud required more than twenty-five procedures to remove various nonmalignant growths. "Thus in 1926," Max Schur says, "there began an endless cycle of leukoplakia, proliferation, precancerous lesions. Each of them had to be treated surgically, by excision, electrocoagulation, or a combination of both." For all these years, Freud constantly suffered pain, sometimes mild, sometimes moderate, sometimes more. His response to that pain was to take some aspirin, to smoke another cigar, and to keep working. After virtually every procedure, Freud jumped back to life: in a day or two he was seeing patients and at his desk again.

Now, in London, in 1938, Schur and Pichler encountered what they took to be another flare-up of the cancer—which would make it the first actual malignancy in fifteen years—and Pichler operated. Freud took a general anesthetic called Evipan, an equivalent, Schur says, of sodium pentathol, and continued with nitrous oxide through a nasal catheter. Pichler was compelled to split Freud's lip and carry the incision up along his nose to get full access to the new lesion. The surgeon used a needle to excise the tumor on the cheek, and found the tissue that he removed was very hard, more like scar tissue than he had expected. When Pichler was sure that he had taken out everything that could be toxic, he inserted the prosthesis and packed the wound cavity with gauze. That night Freud was already up and reading. As it turned out, the tissue that Pichler removed was precancerous, making Exner, one of Freud's British specialists, and Schur wonder if the whole procedure had been necessary at all.

Necessary or not, the operation was brutal, and despite Freud's apparent good health on the night of September 8, recovery was slow and hard. A month later, Freud wrote that he was still not able to work, to sleep well, or to speak as he would like. Nor could he, he confessed, smoke, at least not with any ease. He told Marie Bonaparte that "this operation was the worst since 1923 and has taken a great deal out of me. I am dreadfully tired, and feel weak when I move. I have actually started work with three patients, but it isn't easy. The aftereffects are supposed to be over in six weeks, and I am only at the end of the fourth." As miserable as Freud felt physically, he might have taken some pleasure from the fact that he was still an esteemed figure in England: a score of newspapers carried stories about his operation.

Four days after Freud's operation, Adolf Hitler delivered a fierce denunciation of the Czechs at a party rally in Nuremberg. The terms of abuse were not unlike those that he had used to make way for the Austrian invasion. The German minority in

Czechoslovakia was being roundly persecuted, their rights violated at every turn. Hitler was demanding that the Czechs cede the Sudetenland, where most of the nation's Germans lived. England and France both had strong interests in the Czech situation: France was bound by treaty to declare war if Germany attacked. And now Hitler was testing, as he had in Austria, to find out if the Western powers would rise against him. Some members of the German General Staff were distraught, fearful that Hitler was going to ruin them all, but the führer claimed that he knew the leaders of the Western democracies better than they knew themselves.

Neville Chamberlain, the British prime minister, decided that the best course was to negotiate with Hitler, and so on September 15 he flew to the airfield in Munich. When the Czechs heard the news, they were overwhelmed: they had declared martial law; they had put down agitation by the Germans in the Sudeten; they were ready to stand up against the Nazis. But now, one of their two most potent allies was going off to entreat Hitler on his own territory. The first thing that Chamberlain heard when he landed in Germany was a radio broadcast demanding the immediate annexation of the Sudeten areas to the Reich. Then, much as Schuschnigg had done six months before, Chamberlain went off to meet Hitler at Berchtesgaden. Chamberlain sat and listened to Hitler tell him how modest his designs were. Said Chamberlain after the conference, "In spite of the hardness and ruthlessness I thought I saw in his face, I got the impression that here was a man who could be relied upon when he had given his word."

Soon after, Hitler spoke in Berlin and announced that the Czechs would have to clear out of the Sudetenland by September 26, at which point the land would become a part of Greater Germany. "This is the last territorial claim I have to make in Europe!" Hitler declared.

A conference in Munich at the close of the month involved the nations that Churchill called the Big Four—England, France, Germany, and Italy. But the Czechs themselves had no representation. The Czech diplomats stood outside the door and waited as their powerful friends, the two democracies, did what they were willing to do to defend Czechoslovakia against the fascists. When the meeting among the four ended, the Czechs learned that Hitler would have his way completely. All of the Sudetenland was to be given over to the Germans, with the territory to be evacuated within five days, beginning on October 1. A few days before the Munich Accord, Chamberlain said, "How horrible, fantastic, incredible it is that we should be digging trenches and trying on gas masks here because of a quarrel in a far away country between people of whom we know nothing."

Chamberlain returned to England and cheering crowds, who lined the road on his way back from the airport. Londoners wept in gratitude and relief: their city was not going to be a second Guernica. Chamberlain waved the treaty terms from the window at Downing Street and claimed that he had secured "peace with honor." Then came the line that would become famous: "I believe it is peace for our time."

In his journal on September 30, 1938, Freud scrawled the word "Peace." A few days later, he wrote to Marie Bonaparte,

"Everything here is rather strange, difficult and often bewildering, but all the same it is the only country that we can live in, France being impossible on account of the language. During the days when war seemed imminent the behavior on all sides was exemplary, and it is wonderful to see how now that the intoxication of peace has subsided, people as well as parliament are coming back to their senses and facing the painful truth. We too of course are thankful for the bit of peace, but we cannot take any pleasure in it."

The Munich Accord probably saved Adolf Hitler's life. Many of his senior officers were sure that Germany was not prepared for an all-out war with England and France. A group of them were so distressed that they put together a plot to arrest Hitler and the other leading Nazis and to take over the government themselves. But seeing Hitler's great success at Munich, the plotters backed off and the plan came to nothing. At last convinced that Hitler was the man he said he was, the army fell in behind him. The German population became yet more enraptured with the savior, who seemed able to perform miracles.

Carl Jung, breathless when he contemplated the führer, said, "I saw pictures taken of him in the Czechoslovakian crisis; there was in his eyes the look of a seer. . . . Hitler is the mirror of every German's unconscious. . . . He is the loudspeaker which magnifies the inaudible whispers of the German soul until they can be heard by the German's unconscious ear." Then comes Jung's pronouncement: "Hitler's power is not political; it is *magic*."

*   *   *

On September 27, Freud moved into the house that would always be associated with his memory, 20 Maresfield Gardens in London. "Far too beautiful for us," Freud said of his new address, and it was indeed a lovely house, especially after Ernst finished fitting it out for his mother and father. The price for the house was steep, sixty-five hundred pounds. Freud secured a loan for four thousand from Barclays Bank and soon began worrying about how he would manage to pay it off. One of the reasons—but far from the only one—that Freud was eager to sell an American edition of the Moses book was to help pay down his considerable mortgage.

The house had eight bedrooms, three bathrooms, and two garages. There were gardens at the front and in back, as well as a lawn for playing tennis. (A brochure produced five years before Freud moved in mentions that a few of the rooms had space for a billiard table—not Sigmund Freud's game, alas.) It was a brick house, and though built in 1920, it looked older. The architect, Albert Hastilow, designed it in a revivalist style and Ernst Freud described it as neo-Georgian. The house was sedate and comfortable, and it offered modern appurtenances including gas, electric lights and power, a telephone, constant hot water, and a system of partial—Freud would soon find it far too partial—heating.

Freud called the new house "incomparably better" than Berggasse 19 and declared that he was going "from poverty to white bread" in a stroke. Ernst, he observed, had been busy ruining the house in order to restore it. Freud's son worked to install a lift so that Freud, who was too frail still to manage the stairs, could be transported from one floor to another. But

Ernst's major innovation was to have the wall knocked out between two rooms downstairs, so as to give Freud a large area that would serve as both study and consulting room. This was a sun-brightened space, unlike Freud's darker precincts at Berggasse 19, and here Freud would be able to sit at his desk, brood, talk, answer his correspondence, and make notations in his diary as the light poured in.

But there was still the matter of Freud's furniture: his books, his antiquities, his paintings, and his carpets, all the things that in Vienna had made Freud's sanctum what it was. Freud, skeptical about all human endeavors, with the possible exception of those that he undertook himself, was not at all sure that the Nazis would release his property. He had paid all the taxes and duties, unjust as they were, and yet, as he observed, the Nazi gangsters were not a predictable lot. When Freud heard that his things were actually packed, he simply said, "There's many a slip between cup and lip."

At the end of the first week of August, Freud's shipment had arrived and now, moving into Maresfield Gardens, he could begin to restore his old life. Here was his library, or at least the balance of it. (Before he left Vienna, he had been compelled to part with about eight hundred volumes, which eventually turned up in New York City.) Here was the famous couch, a gift from an early patient, a Mrs. Benvenisti, who presented him with it in 1891. And, most warming to Freud surely, here was his collection of antiquities, fully intact. For the past few months, he had been forced to subsist on his terra-cottas; on the gifts that people, sometimes strangers who knew all about his love for these works, kindly sent his way; and of course on the statue of Athena that Marie Bonaparte had smuggled out of Vienna for him.

Now Freud had his picture of the great physician Charcot, one of his first inspirations, to hang over the couch. He had his rendering of the Roman forum, by Luigi Kasimir, which would recall to Freud his intense, abiding interest in archaeology and his conviction that the mind was structured like a grand archaeological site, with city on top of ruined city, memory atop memory. Now Freud had his rather bland bust of that anonymous Roman citizen, which, for whatever reason, he gave pride of place to, posing it on a column of its own. He had his photographs of the erotic trinity, the two of Marie Bonaparte, and one each of Lou Andreas-Salomé and of Yvette Guilbert, who would actually come and visit Freud at Maresfield Gardens when she was in London in 1939 for her three performances at Wigmore Hall.

Freud not only had his desk, but the anthropomorphically shaped chair designed to make Freud comfortable, or as comfortable as possible, when he twisted his body up to read. Now Freud had access to the portraits of some of the men he thought of as his masters: Hermann Helmholtz, the arch-materialist; Ernst Brücke; and Ernst von Fleischl-Marxou. In the middle of it all sat Freud, like a monarch whose kingdom had, late in his life, been restored to him.

*   *   *

Yet from his new, light-drenched study, Freud was forced to contemplate events that were anything but lovely. On November 7, a seventeen-year-old Polish Jew named Herschel Grynszpan, who had grown up in Germany, learned that his parents had been deported from Germany to Poland. Grynszpan, living in Paris at the time, got himself a revolver, walked into the German embassy, and shot the first official he met. Ernst vom Rath, third secretary of the German embassy, was badly wounded. Goebbels exploited the event for all it was worth. The Nazi newspapers described the shooting as an attack launched by something called "world Jewry" against the integrity of the Reich. The papers promised "the heaviest consequences" for German Jews.

Late in the afternoon of November 9, Hitler learned that Ernst vom Rath was dead and almost immediately issued orders to Goebbels for a full-scale attack on all Jews living in the Reich. Hitler also informed Goebbels that the death of the Nazi diplomat would be the excuse for seizing available Jewish assets and for exiling the Jews from as many aspects of German life as possible. Quickly the orders went out to set about burning synagogues and destroying Jewish homes. One typical set of instructions ran this way: "A Jew has fired a shot. A German diplomat is dead. In Friedrichstadt, Kiel, Lubeck and elsewhere there are completely superfluous meeting houses. These people still have shops amongst us too. Both are superfluous. There must be no looting. There must be no manhandling. Foreign Jews must not be touched. The action must be carried out in civilian clothing and be concluded by 5 a.m."

Many of the storm troopers who received such orders were still in their beer halls, celebrating the fifteenth anniversary of Hitler's attempted putsch of 1923. They were in no condition to be told not to manhandle anyone and not to loot. Almost immediately, the brownshirts hit the streets, carrying clubs and knives and swinging cans of gasoline. Soon nearly every synagogue in Germany was burning. By the end of the night almost a thousand were destroyed. The Germans also went from Jewish shop to Jewish shop, smashing the windows, and leaving the sidewalks inches deep in broken glass. Thus the evening acquired its name, Kristallnacht, the Night of the Broken Glass. Of the nine thousand Jewish-owned shops in Germany, the Nazis destroyed seventy-five hundred that night. In some places, storm troopers went to Jewish cemeteries and smashed the gravestones. In Esslington, brownshirts forced their way into the Jewish orphanage, broke the furniture, and destroyed the books while the children watched, in tears.

In Saarbrücken the Jews were compelled to dance outside their synagogue, and to sing religious songs; then the Nazis drenched them with water and left them standing in the frozen air. In Essen, storm troopers set the beards of Jewish men on fire. In Meppen, Jewish men were forced to kiss the ground in front of SA headquarters, and while they did, brownshirts kicked them and walked over them. In many cities and towns Jews had to wear placards proclaiming that they were the murderers of vom Rath. By the time it was over, between one and two thousand Jews were dead, three hundred had, or would soon, commit suicide, and thirty thousand had been arrested and taken off to Dachau, Buchenwald, and Sachsenhausen. Summarizing the events of Kristallnacht in the *Racial Observer*, Goebbels said, "The German people are an anti-semitic people. They take no pleasure or delight in allowing themselves to be provoked as a nation by the parasitic Jewish race."

In Vienna, where the same violent protocols were observed that night, the Nazis got their hands on Freud. Arthur Freud was a professor, fifty-six years old at the time; he was a journalist in Vienna and held a passport from Czechoslovakia. In the morning, he walked out to a Jewish community center, hoping to get more information on the events of the day, and believing that his foreign passport would protect him. At the center, Professor Freud encountered a detachment of Nazis who politely let him pass. But once inside, he met another one and they attacked. The commanding officer grabbed him by the shirt and demanded to know who and what he was. When the professor gave his name, there came a cry of triumph: "Now they have him!" And for a while the Nazis did in fact believe that they had apprehended Sigmund Freud.

Finally, the troopers released Arthur Freud, who went home that night and had his apartment searched by two more Nazi thugs, pretending that they were looking for weapons. What they did find were some works by Sigmund Freud's Viennese nemesis, Karl Kraus, who had died in 1936. One of the Nazis commanded Freud to burn them because, he insisted, "that one was the biggest Jewish filthy fellow." Though Sigmund Freud probably never learned anything about the fate of his namesake on Kristallnacht, he was well aware of events. "Pogroms in Germany," he wrote in his diary.

After Kristallnacht, Jews throughout Germany and what had been Austria fled in great numbers. But they did not always have an easy time of it. An ocean liner called the *Saint Louis* left Hamburg with about a thousand German Jews onboard, all of whom had permission to enter the United States—not immediately, but in either 1940 or 1941. The ship docked in Cuba, where the refugees hoped that they could stay until they became eligible to enter the States, but Cuba would not allow them to come ashore. Nor would Argentina, Brazil, Chile, Colombia, Panama, Paraguay, or Uruguay take a single one of the Jews. Soon the ship was passing back and forth along the Florida coastline as the American government debated whether to offer refuge or not. The answer was no; and with that, the *Saint Louis* could do nothing but turn around and make its way back to Europe. The boat docked in Antwerp and the refugees went off to various nearby countries, including France, Belgium, and Holland, all of which were soon overrun by the Nazis, who visited on many of the passengers from the *Saint Louis* the predictable fate.

But not every nation—or every person—turned away from the survivors of Kristallnacht. "Many of those in Britain," Martin Gilbert says, "who took in Jewish children after Kristallnacht hardly had the resources to do so, but wanted to help, and willingly accepted the hardships involved. In Archway, North London"—not far from Freud—"Miss Harder, who ran a sweet and tobacconist shop, and lived in a two bedroom flat, took in two sisters who reached London from Prague on June 2. Six months after taking them in, she died of tuberculosis. But during the short time she looked after them, she took them on holiday, on the Isle of Wight, at her own expense, and tried—in vain—to get their mother out of Czechoslovakia."

Freud responded to the events of early November 1938 in part by publishing a letter on anti-Semitism in *Time and Tide*. "I came to Vienna as a child of four years," he wrote, "from a small town in Moravia. After seventy-eight years of assiduous work I had to leave my home, saw the scientific society I had founded dissolved, our institutions destroyed, our printing press ("Verlag") taken over by the invaders, the books I had published confiscated or reduced to pulp, my children expelled from their professions." All was true and all grievous enough. But then Freud adds something surprising: "Don't you think," he asks the editors, "you ought to reserve the columns of your special number for the utterances of non-Jewish people, less personally involved than myself?" What Freud hoped for, it's clear, was for others—for gentiles—to speak out against Nazi barbarity, rather than leaving that task to the Jews, who could be seen simply as protecting their own interests. What the Nazis were doing was bad enough to anger any sane and civil person, so why should the Jews have to be in the forefront of protest?

The brief letter to *Time and Tide* echoes a piece that Freud published two weeks before Kristallnacht: his "Comment on Anti-Semitism." There, Freud says that he is drawing from an essay by another writer, though Freud cannot remember precisely who it is. The unremembered writer, whom the reader presumes to be a gentile, does the work of defending the Jews and in their behalf says some rather flattering things. "The Jews are not worse than we are; they have somewhat other characteristics and somewhat other faults, but on the whole we have no right to look down on them. In some respects, indeed, they are our superiors. They do not need so much alcohol as we do in order to make life tolerable; crimes of brutality, murder, robbery, and sexual violence are great rarities among them; they have always set a high value on intellectual achievement and interests; their family life is more intimate; they take better care of the poor; charity is a sacred duty to them."

The writer whose voice and thoughts Freud is borrowing is Mark Twain and the essay is called "Concerning the Jews," which Twain published in *Harper's Magazine*. Some of the things that Twain goes on to say in his so-called defense of the Jews are a little less palatable than the lines that Freud re-members and adapts. The Jew, Twain says, "has a reputation for various small forms of cheating and for practicing oppressive usury, and for burning himself out to get the insurance, and for arranging cunning contracts which leave him an exit but lock the other man in, and for smart evasions which find him safe and comfortable just within the strict letter of the law, when court and jury know very well that he has violated the spirit of it."

Yet even had he recalled this passage, Freud might have been forgiving, for he dearly loved Twain's work and even went to see him perform in Vienna once, where Twain told a story about stealing a watermelon that Freud remembered for a long time and eventually used to illustrate a point in *Civilization and Its Discontents*. Twain, in fact, spent a few years in Vienna when he was at the height of his fame (hotels offered reduced rates to have him on hand) and Freud was a relative unknown. Had the two ever met—there is no evidence that they did—they could have taken up a mutual favorite subject: both strongly doubted that William Shakespeare had written the magnificent works with which the world credited him.

The defenses of the Jews that Freud made in his letter to *Time and Tide* and in the short essay where he borrowed from Twain are not, strictly speaking, Freudian pieces of writing. They are civic and thoughtful. They don't investigate the strange passions that give rise to racial hatred; they don't attempt to shock the reader with new insights. Be decent, they say—and little more. They are the work of a public man addressing public issues in a clear-minded, humane way. Freud's deeper, more arresting ideas on the hatred Jews could generate was at the center of his new work, the book on Moses.

Over time, Freud was becoming something of a monument in Maresfield Gardens. Everyone with literary or cultural aspirations in London, it seemed, needed an audience with him. Ernest Jones and Anna did what they could to shield him from the pressure of his new fame, but they did not always succeed: Freud was too important, too esteemed—and maybe even loved.

A hundred or so years before, another figure had ensconced himself in a dwelling not so far from 20 Maresfield Gardens. In the latter part of his career, Samuel Taylor Coleridge became the sage of Highgate. His great poems—"The Rime of the Ancient Mariner," "Kubla Khan," "Christabel," and the rest—were well behind him. He lived with the kindly physician James

Gilman, who managed Coleridge's opium supply (or tried) and helped the greatest literary talent of the age—according to many; sometimes even according to Coleridge himself—to impose a measure of regularity on what had been a rather dissolute life. Coleridge at Highgate became part of the grand tour. Young men like Ralph Waldo Emerson and Thomas Carlyle presented themselves for an audience with the magus. Some time well after noon, Coleridge trundled into the parlor and began holding forth on anything from the linguistic theories of Horne Tooke to the strange and probably inexplicable vagaries of his digestion—opium having a peculiar effect on the belly and the bowels.

By this time, Coleridge had become an intellectual pillar of the existing order. He wrote on behalf of the established church and the ruling state. His work became a cornerstone of conservative political and social theory. If he never quite renounced his earlier scandalous, sometimes terrifying, poetry—the influence of which in time traveled everywhere, from Poe to the multiplex cinema—he had left all that far behind. Now STC, as he preferred to be called, wrote little verse. In his premature old age, the sage of Highgate turned away from what was most rich and strange in himself and became an ever-talkative, ever-blander public man.

The question now was whether the sage of Maresfield Gardens would wither into respectability the way that Coleridge did. Like Coleridge, Freud received a great number of visitors: Arnold Zweig came, stayed a fortnight, and left with an apology to Freud for tiring him out; H. G. Wells, who tried unsuccessfully to get British citizenship for Freud and was one of the few who dared call Freud by his surname, also turned up; and naturally, the princess came: she visited nearly ten times and her presence was each time greatly treasured by Freud. There had been Dalí with his fears about the death of surrealism; Yahuda had come with his anxieties about the Moses book. Though prone now to deafness, Freud gave all his visitors a measure of rather serene attention. He was far from having the strength to deliver Coleridgean monologues, not that he had ever had such an inclination very often. He spoke his mind in compressed sentences, exhibited courtly, old-world manners, and did his best to keep his guests occupied.

One of the more intriguing visits to Freud was from Leonard and Virginia Woolf. Virginia was arguably the preeminent British novelist of the time; her husband, Leonard, was a journalist, a political theorist, and the director of the Hogarth Press, which had been publishing Freud's books in English translation and would soon sponsor James Strachey's grand Standard Edition. Leonard was gaunt, hyperintellectual, pipe-smoking; Virginia still beautiful, high-strung, and—to both herself and others—sometimes almost unbearably perceptive. On Saturday, January 28, 1939, they went to have tea with Freud at 20 Maresfield Gardens. "Nearly all famous men are disappointing or bores, or both," Leonard recalls in his memoir. "Freud was neither; he had an aura, not of fame, but of greatness. . . . It was not an easy interview. He was extraordinarily courteous in a formal, old-fashioned way—for instance, almost ceremoniously he presented Virginia with a flower." The flower was a narcissus, a strange enough gift, given Freud's ideas about the female proclivity for narcissism and Woolf's repudiation of such thoughts—to her, men were by far the greater practitioners of self-love. "There was something about him," Leonard continues, "as of a half-extinct volcano, something somber, suppressed, reserved. He gave me the feeling which only very few people whom I have met gave me, a feeling of great gentleness, but behind the gentleness, great strength."

They sat down for tea in Freud's consulting room, which seemed to Leonard "almost a museum," and they talked, naturally, about Hitler. Virginia expressed a sense of guilt, saying that if the Allies had not won the war of 1914, there might have been no Nazis and no Hitler. Virginia's idea was a form of the notion, which has not disappeared, that it was the mistreatment of Germany at Versailles, by France in particular, that had led to the current crises. Freud disagreed. Hitler and the Nazis would still have come and they would have been yet worse if the Germans had won the war.

Leonard, who was not always the most tactful of men, went on to tell Freud a story. He described a recent court case in which a man was convicted of stealing a number of books from Foyle's, including a volume of Freud's. The magistrate who heard the case fined the man, but he expressed another wish for the thief's punishment. According to Leonard, the magistrate wanted to sentence the man to the reading of all of Freud's work.

Freud was amused, or so Leonard claims, and self-deprecatory about his own achievements. "My books have made me infamous," Freud said, "not famous." Yet what perhaps allowed Freud to say as much was how famous he had now become, at least in London. One exception to the consenus about Freud's greatness seems to have been Virginia Woolf, whose account of the afternoon is rather different from Leonard's. She recalled Freud as "a screwed up shrunk very old man: with a monkeys light eyes, paralyzed spasmodic movements, inarticulate: but alert." Later she added that "all refugees are like gulls with their beaks out for possible crumbs." Anna Freud was developing a book, Martin hoped to place a novel—and they made the error of asking Virginia for advice.

Perhaps before they left, Leonard and Virginia Woolf told Freud the story of Mitz the marmoset, for it was surely one that Freud would have relished. In 1935, the Woolfs went off on a driving tour of Western Europe in Leonard's Lanchester 18 car, which had a Tickford roof that retracted to leave the vehicle completely open. With them, they took Mitz, Leonard's pet marmoset, who often sat perched on his master's shoulder. One day, in Germany, the Woolfs found themselves driving into a crowd. The road was lined with Nazis in uniform and school-children carrying swastika flags. The people were drawn up very closely on both sides awaiting the arrival of some high Nazi official, and Leonard had to drive quite slowly through them. Leonard, who was a Jew, was naturally worried about what was going to happen next.

"We were closely penned in," he said, "by what . . . seemed to be an unending procession of enthusiastic Nazis. But we soon found that there was no need for us to worry. It was a very warm day and I was driving with the car open; on my shoulder sat Mitz. I had to drive at about fifteen miles an hour. When they saw Mitz the crowd shrieked with delight. Mile after mile I drove between the two lines of corybantic Germans, and the whole way they shouted 'Heil Hitler! Heil Hitler!' to Mitz and

gave her (and secondarily Virginia and me) the Hitler salute
with outstretched arm."

Surely the most surprising figure to pass through Freud's London
life was Doctor Anton Sauerwald, the Nazi commissioner who
handled Freud's case in Vienna, and who turned up in London
early in October of 1938. His name is inscribed in Freud's diary,
which is what Freud usually did after receiving a visitor, and yet
there seems to be no other evidence of a meeting between Freud
and his former oppressor turned advocate. Max Schur attests to the
fact that Sauerwald did go and visit Freud's brother, Alexander.

By now, it was clear to the Freud family that Sauerwald had
saved Freud from serious trouble by holding back information
about his finances and particularly his overseas bank accounts
from the Nazis. Alexander asked him about this directly. "The
Führer," Sauerwald replied, "who of course knows best, realizes
that the fatherland is in a state of siege. The Jews, due to their
internationalist leanings and their tendency toward individua-
listic behavior, cannot form a reliable element of the population.
Thus they have to be eliminated. This might be deplored, but
the end justifies the means. This does not mean, however, that
an individual should not be permitted to alleviate individual
hardship in selected cases."

Max Schur came to suspect that Sauerwald was in England as
a spy. But given Freud's current standing, it is possible that at
least one reason for Sauerwald's trip was to pay homage to the
great and good man who had deeply moved his Nazi heart. By

his own later account, Sauerwald came to London by Freud's invitation to discuss various financial matters. Sauerwald went on to claim that during the visit, Freud asked him to arrange for Pichler, the surgeon, to come and to examine him as soon as was reasonably possible. Sauerwald said that he did as much, even going so far as to roll the expense of the visit into "moving expenses" and thus save Freud an extra payment.

In his postwar trial for war crimes, Sauerwald gave himself credit for attempting to save the books in stock at the Verlag by an agreement with Marie Bonaparte, which alas fell through at the last moment. Nonetheless, he said, he did manage to get the books out of Vienna and distributed to numerous universities all through Europe. He also said that he convinced the director of the Austrian National Library, Paul Heigl, to have the library store boxes of books that contained nearly all the volumes that the Verlag had issued. After the war, when Anton Sauerwald went on trial, Anna Freud and Marie Bonaparte wrote letters in his behalf, describing his services to the Freud family and entreating the court for mercy, which in fact was granted.

It is not all clear how much of what Sauerwald recounts about his trip to London is to be believed. Perhaps he did admire Freud; perhaps he did take an interest in psychoanalysis, but the bomb maker who so efficiently investigated his own explosions seems to have had one salient talent in life: the ability to play both sides of the game. Nothing that the commissioner ever did should escape the assumption that some form of duplicity was involved.

*　　*　　*

Amid all the adulation that Freud received in London, there was one discordant sound. Freud received endless advice—sometimes it was closer to warning—not to publish the Moses book. Charles Singer, a distinguished historian of science, pleaded with Freud, through his son Ernst, to suppress the manuscript. To Singer, Freud wrote, "I have spent my whole life standing up for what I have considered to be the scientific truth, even when it was uncomfortable and unpleasant for my fellow men. I cannot end up with an act of disavowal. Your letter contains the assurance which testifies to your superior intelligence, that everything I write is bound to cause misunderstanding—and—may I add—indignation. Well, we Jews have been reproached for growing cowardly in the course of centuries. (Once upon a time we were a valiant nation.) In this transformation I had no share. So I must risk it."

Finally for Freud, the time of ease and acceptance—of intoxication—ended, and all warnings assimilated but none obeyed, he sent *Moses and Monotheism* out into the world. On Thursday, February 2, 1939, Allert de Lange, in Amsterdam, printed the book in German. A month or so later, Freud received two copies from Holland; one he kept, the other he gave to Princess Bonaparte.

What Freud wanted most now was to see his volume come out in English and exactly as he had conceived it. He chided Ernest Jones and his wife, Katherine, for being too slow and slack with the translation. (Jones may have been many things, but he was never slack.) And Freud also pressed Leonard Woolf to make sure the book would come out in English exactly as Freud wished. When Woolf wrote to

Freud and asked him if the Hogarth Press might change the book's title and call it simply "Moses," because the longer word, "monotheism," would scare off readers, Freud, "nice man" that he was, shot back that there would be no such change. He even wrote ahead to his American publisher, Knopf, to say that the title of his book would be *Moses and Monotheism*, and that was that. On May 19 Freud had the satisfaction of seeing his long-pondered, already much-criti-cized work in the language of his new country. The deed was done: as Peter Gay says, Freud "had conceived his *Moses and Monotheism* in defiance, written it in defiance, published it in defiance."

The most immediately scandalous parts of *Moses and Mono-theism* were Freud's reflections on the identity of Moses. "To deprive a people of the man whom they take pride in," says Freud on the book's opening page, "is not a thing to be gladly or carelessly undertaken, least of all by someone who is himself one of them." To prove the point that Moses was an Egyptian and not a Jew—if in fact he did prove it or come close—Freud drew on a couple of possibilities. The name Moses, he asserted, was not a Jewish one, as scholarship had long understood, but Egyptian. Then too, Freud said, the biblical story of Moses's origins does not make psychoanalytical sense. In that most common of fantasies, which Freud called the "family romance," the child believes that though he may live with a humble family, his true parents are well-to-do aristocrats, perhaps even a king and a queen, from whom he was separated early in life. The biblical story about Moses being rescued by an Egyptian princess reverses the usual direction of the family romance: in it the child goes not from wealth to poverty, but from poverty to wealth. This fact provokes Freud's analytic interest. "In every instance which it has been possible to test," he says, "the first family, the one from which the child was exposed, was the invented one, and the second one, in which he was received and grew up, was the real one." In the Moses story, the first family is the poor family of Jews, the second family is Egyptian. So, Freud declares Moses must have started out as an upper-class Egyptian and somehow been taken up and adopted by impoverished Jews.

Then there is the matter of the origins of monotheism. Drawing on his anthropological and archaeological researches, Freud speculates that monotheism was not a Jewish, but rather an Egyptian invention. It was Amenhotep IV, not Moses or any other Jew, who converted to the monotheistic cult of Aton and began to spread the command to worship one god. Amenhotep, according to Freud, changed his name to Ikhnaton and attempted to impose his severe religion on the Egyptian polytheists. Moses was originally one of Ikhnaton's closest associates, but Ikhnaton died young, the Egyptians refused monotheism, and Moses turned instead to the Jews, who had been in Egypt for a few generations. He led the Jews out of Egypt, defying the pharaoh, and in the desert gave them laws, introduced them to circumcision, which had been an Egyptian custom, and persuaded them to worship Aton.

The Jews eventually repudiated Moses and Aton: the worship of one god was too cold and abstract for them. Angry because of all he has asked them to relinquish, they killed Moses and then lapsed back into their old forms of polytheism. Yet the memory of Moses and his religion persisted. The Jews felt remorse for what they had done, and that remorse exalted Moses's memory—what Freud calls a "reaction formation" took place. Slowly, a Midianite tribal god lost his violent qualities until he was nearly identical to the old Mosaic god, Aton, and so became, accordingly, the precursor for Yahweh. The repressed returned—in the form of monotheism—and the slain Moses came to be Judaism's great man.

One would be hard put to argue that these ideas are among Freud's most astute or grounded. Freud was letting his mind roam; he was speculating, guessing. And this is where many of Freud's perceptions come from, his best and worst alike. Freud got ideas in part because he was so open to them. He wrote them down for better and worse, and he let the bad take him to the good, and sometimes the good to the bad. The reader of Freud often has to do some work: in Freud's richest, strangest volumes, the reader occasionally has to play the part of ego to Freud's creative id, and sift matters out, see what might be true, what not. Early in his career as a consequential writer—which means in the middle of his life—Freud quoted Schiller on the philosophy of composition. Open it all up, the poet says. Let it run. Only once you've allowed the unconscious to express itself should you bring your judgment into play. Or as Saul Bellow, in his way an heir of Schiller's romanticism, puts it, "Everybody knows there is no finesse or accuracy of suppression; if you hold down one thing you hold down the adjoining."

Moses was not a Jew but an Egyptian; the Egyptian's were the first to disseminate the idea of there being one god and one only; the Chosen People murdered their greatest prophet. These are, perhaps, the kinds of perceptions Freud allowed in so as not to hold down the adjoining ones. And in fact in its deeper precincts, *Moses and Monotheism* is one of Freud's most illuminating books. Yet the public headed immediately for what was most vulnerable and least valuable about the work.

The reviews and early responses to the Moses book were generally about as furious and uncomprehending as Freud anticipated. Martin Buber, the formidable Jewish theologian, would sneer at the book as "regrettable" and "groundless." To Abraham Yahuda, the thoughtful neighbor on Elsworthy Road, who enjoined Freud not to publish at all, the book could have been the work of a Christian fanatic out to malign the Jews. Peter Gay quotes one Father McNabb, who, in London's *Catholic Herald*, wondered how long "free, generous England" would continue to extend a welcome to the author of so scandalous a work. Freud, the pious father claimed, was a champion not only of atheism (as he surely was), but also of incest. The reviewer for the *New York Times* closed by observing that Freud's "flimsy theories, which in part involve an interweaving of those he admits borrowing from others, are not the type of 'knowledge' that is worth the misunderstanding and the ill will that it is more than likely to breed at this time." An anonymous letter from the United States observed that it was regrettable that the German gangsters had not put Freud in a concentration camp, which was surely where he belonged. A writer in Palestine called Freud an "*Am Haaretz*," a bumptious know-nothing.

Freud's response was characteristic enough. He reveled in the book's strong sales figures—by June of 1939 it had sold 1,800 copies in its German edition—and he took the criticism in his stride. Now eighty-three years old, so sick that he had trouble walking and in constant pain, he still had the stuff for a fight.

Surely the sense of safety and contentment that Freud acquired when he first came to London and was greeted with flowers and gifts was now diminished. What Freud would have called the social superego stood in a much more complex and fraught relation to him. Any sense of inner unity and calm that Freud experienced during the halcyon early days in free, liberal England was now compromised. Freud was once again the person who caused trouble. He was the one who caught the middle-class asleep and stirred it up. Once again, Freud was the author of *The Interpretation of Dreams* and *Three Essays on the Theory of Sexuality*, books that caused upset in readers and brought conflict to Freud. Once again he could claim to be, as he told the Woolfs, not famous but infamous. The publication of the Moses book must have made Freud anxious, as conflict does, and it must have infused him with some energy, for conflict does that too. And by returning Freud to his early days of mental fight, as Blake would call it, the publication of *Moses and Monotheism* probably did something else too. It probably made Freud feel, for however brief a span of time, as though he was again young. "An aged man is but a paltry thing, / A tattered coat upon a stick." So far true enough, perhaps. But Yeats adds something more: "An aged man is but a paltry thing, / A tattered coat upon a stick, unless / Soul clap its hands and sing, and louder sing / For every tatter in its mortal dress."

"Quite a worthy exit," Freud himself said of the Moses book in a letter to Hanns Sachs, which was true enough.

At a certain point, pain became Sigmund Freud's element; it was a constant factor in his life, like the air he was breathing. After the operation that Pichler performed in September of 1938, Freud suffered constantly from pain in his jaw and related complications. Winter came on, and the weather was cold; the house at Maresfield Gardens, elegantly appointed as it may have been, was drafty, and this of course increased Freud's discomfort. At the end of January, Freud complained of an acute ache in his jaw. It turned out that a chip of bone, left in after Pichler's operation in September, was causing irritation. Schur removed it, but in the process he encountered more swelling in the back of Freud's mouth. This time, it looked to Schur like a malignancy.

The next month, Freud wrote to Max Eitingon to say that he had developed "a strong antipathy" toward his supposed savior, Doctor Pichler. Freud was referring overtly to the months of bone ache he had suffered, but perhaps indirectly to his exasperation with Pichler for prolonging a life that was more and more arduous. Yet as a rule, Freud would still not take any medication stronger than aspirin. Though he was writing little, if at all, for publication, Freud continued to read plentifully, to compose letters, to receive guests, and to conduct therapy; for these things, he needed his mind to be clear.

Late in February of 1939, Freud had X-rays taken of the right side of his face and head, the cancerous side. They were presided over by Doctor Lacassagne, whom the princess brought from Paris expressly for the purpose. It was Lacassagne who, a few years before, helped to save Princess Bonaparte's dog, Topsy. The X-ray that Lacassagne took depicts Freud's skull in a soft, luminous white against a shaded background. There, toward the rear of his jaw, is a large, irregular hole—it looks like the site of a bomb blast—where once there had been teeth, gums, and bone. The X-ray makes the jaw look like what it was, a gaping hole of pain. Some tissue was taken as well and the biopsy revealed what Freud expected, more malignancy, more cancer. And now there could be no further surgery— assuming Freud would have consented to suffer through yet another operation—because the cancer was much too close to Freud's eye socket and perhaps even too close to his brain. After the X-rays, Freud wrote to his younger friend Arnold Zweig, "I have had some unpleasant weeks, not just being ill and in pain, but also complete indecision about the next steps to be taken. Operation and radium treatment (Paris) were finally abandoned and an external application of Roentgen ray was decided on; this is due to start tomorrow. (There is now no further doubt that I have a new recurrence of my dear old cancer with which I have been sharing my existence for sixteen years. At that time naturally no one could predict which of us would prove the stronger.)"

The X-ray regimen was brutal: Freud lost the beard from the right side of his face; he got headaches, became dizzy; he bled from the right side of his mouth. Yet nonetheless, Freud continued to see his patients. Finzi, another one of Freud's physicians, would eventually write, that "He absolutely refuses to let us give him any pain relieving medicament of any sort except aspirin." What Freud really needed, the physician said, was psychoanalytic treatment to make him a little saner and so induce him to take some stronger drugs. But of this, Finzi admitted, there was not much hope. Freud detested the X-ray treatment, but observed that it was better than the other salient alternative, which was cutting off his head.

On May 6, 1939, Freud celebrated his eighty-third birthday. He sat for a while in the garden and received birthday greetings from family and friends, which were, as per the Freud family tradition, tied around the necks of the household dogs and sent Freud's way. But Freud could only bear company for so long. He tottered briefly around the garden exchanging greetings, but was soon back inside his study again and trying, insofar as the pain would allow, to get some rest.

Adolf Hitler, Freud's antagonist, had recently observed a birthday himself, albeit under much different circumstances. On April 20, 1939, two weeks before Freud tremblingly opened his birthday messages, Hitler celebrated his fiftieth birthday with an enormous parade. All three branches of the military turned out, as well as the Waffen SS. By the führer's orders, all the latest German armaments were on display: there were tanks, antiaircraft guns, and searchlights. Overhead, air force fighter planes and bombers roared. Back in his retreat, there was a special birthday gift for Hitler. For more than a year, workmen had been laboring away on an elevator that would take the führer from the bottom of the Kehlstein to the mountain's top, so that he could survey his domains. For Hitler's birthday the work was completed. The door to the elevator was plated with gold and inside there were padded seats, carpets, and sophisticated safety devices. But Hitler only went to the mountaintop three times; the air, he complained, was too rare for him there: he could hardly breathe.

After a while, Freud took up residence in the downstairs consulting room and library. He tried to read and to write letters, surrounded by his books and his antiquities; he slept there on the couch, which so many patients had used before him; he looked off into the spacious garden he had come very quickly to love. Anna was his constant nurse and companion (Martha was now in the background; Aunt Minna was too sick to attend well even to herself); Schur lavished all the care he could muster onto his lone, distinguished patient.

When, following Marie Bonaparte's recommendation, Freud took Max Schur on as his doctor in 1929, Freud made Schur promise that he would always be completely honest about Freud's medical condition, however severe it might become. There was another matter too: "Promise me," Freud said, "when the time comes, you won't let them torment me unnecessarily." Schur agreed and the two men shook hands.

In April, Schur took a brief trip to the United States. Planning to emigrate there eventually (one can imagine Freud's verdict on this idea), he took his family over to get them settled as he began the process of acquiring an American medical license. When Schur came back in July, Freud had lost a good deal of weight and he seemed relatively apathetic, at least by his usual standard of intellectual vigor. "I also had the definite impression," Schur said, "that a new carcinomatous ulceration had developed behind and slightly upward of the old lesion, in the direction of the base of the orbita. The bone was extremely tender, and there was a fetid odor."

In one of his most profound essays, "Mourning and Melancholia," Freud suggests that loss is so common and pervasive in life that we may be in the process of mourning almost all the time. If that is so, then Freud's mourning in the last weeks of his life must have been particularly intense, for he was losing a great deal and very rapidly.

One of Freud's first losses was his psychoanalytical practice. This time Freud must have understood that the loss was permanent and not temporary, as it had been when he ceased to see patients in Vienna. On the first day of August, Freud took the step of disbanding what had been a fifty-three-year endeavor. He had worked with Dora and the Rat Man and the Wolf Man and Little Hans, but he had also consulted with hundreds of others, including all of the first-generation of analysts, down to his daughter Anna. (Simply to be a first-generation analyst meant that one had been analyzed by Freud: there was no other central authority.) Freud had begun his career as a medical doctor and often thought of himself foremost as a healer—though to be sure he was many other things. Bringing to bear what remained a formidable intelligence, he now created synopses of each of his current cases for Anna, so that the patients could continue their therapeutic work.

With one case in particular, late in his life, Freud had reportedly become aggravated. When the patient did not make progress after weeks and weeks, Freud cried out in frustration, "You do not think that it is worth your while to love an old man." In the final phase of therapeutic practice—the mode of healing that Freud finally settled upon after trying a number of others—love was, in fact, at the heart of everything. Having made use of hypnotism and free association and dream interpretation, Freud now put himself, the physician, at the center of the drama. Freud became an analyst of what he called "the transference."

Over time, Freud came to the conclusion that his patients were falling in love with him. But he also recognized that they were doing so for reasons that transcended his own charms, such as those might be. For a neurotic individual, Freud asserted (and for almost everyone else, he at times suggested), a new figure who arrives on the scene promising enlightenment, a cure, the truth, love, will activate a spectrum of childhood emotions. The patient will transfer feelings once directed to the mother and the father, and later to other figures of authority, onto the person of the doctor. From this transference of feeling, the analyst can learn the dynamics of the patient's erotic life. All the failures and sorrows that have been part of his past relations with objects of desire and of authority will in time be manifest in what Freud thought of as "the theater of the transference." The patient will repeat his old prototypes, with the physician as the object. Freud observes that in therapy "the patient does not *remember* anything of what he has forgotten and repressed, but *acts* it out. He reproduces it not as a memory but as an action; he *repeats* it, without, of course, knowing that he is repeating it."

But finally, because the analyst does not reciprocate, but instead *analyzes* the offering of love from a detached, disciplined position, he can help the patient to see his old frustrating patterns. The patient will be able to apprehend, for instance, how all of his relations with figures of power in his life, no matter how distinct and singular they appear to him to be, are actually repetitions of old prototypes. Perhaps he has always embraced authorities fervently, and then, at a certain point, turned against them with bitter ingratitude. Perhaps all his erotic relations have ended in a certain sort of revulsion and what appears to be an inexplicable loss of sexual interest on his part. In therapy, the consistent patterns of frustration come to the fore, and with the therapist's assistance, they become visible. They become something that the patient comprehends. And with this gain in awareness, there can be change in behavior. By putting self-aware ego where repetitious id had been, the patient acquires some measure of experiential freedom. At the core of Freud's humanism, measured as it generally is, there lies the belief that if a person can describe his inner life with some accuracy—apply words where before there has only been silence and compulsion—then he can be just a little bit freer, and maybe (dare one say it?) a little bit happier than he has been in the past.

"The transference," Freud says, "creates an intermediate region between illness and real life through which the transition from the one to the other is made. The new condition has taken over all the features of the illness; but it represents an artificial illness which is at every point accessible to our intervention." For the cure to begin, though, the patient had to capitulate in the transference; he had to succumb to the allure of the physician.

So from about the midpoint of his career as a therapist, Freud had, day by day, hour by hour, been the object of the most passionate feelings from his patients, both male and female. He had been fiercely and often eloquently desired. But of course, with Eros being the ambivalent force that it is, Freud had been detested too. Within the confines of his magus's lair, amid the carpets and the statues and the overflow of scholarly books, Freud had lived a life of supreme erotic intensity. He had been courted, teased, insulted, worshipped, adored—and, the morning's sessions done, he had repaired to the front of Berggasse 19 for his noon meal, followed by his walk, his purchase of a book or newspaper, his beard trim. Then back again in the afternoon to the labors of Eros. Freud had led the life of a chaste Don Juan—and much like Byron's Don Juan, he had in fact been much more often pursued than pursuing.

But something else is noteworthy about the dynamics of transference analysis as Freud developed it. At the height of the transference, Freud may have been manifest to a given patient as the most magisterial figure of authority imaginable, the ultimate subject who is supposed to know, in Jacques Lacan's useful phrase. But Freud's objective was not to maintain this position. No, the aim of therapy was to demystify absolute authority, which meant, most immediately, to demystify Freud. The patient who is able, at last, to become self-aware about his hunger for unassailable truth and complete love takes up a new relation to all objects of desire and authority in his life, past and future. And he also takes up a new attitude to the analyst, to Freud. By the end of therapy, the patient who has passed through the vale of the transference is able to see Freud the therapist as another suffering, striving mortal, not unlike himself. He might be aware of Freud's high intelligence and his remarkable originality, but because of the analysis, the patient would no longer see Freud as anything like a mortal god.

The ritual of psychoanalytical therapy has at its central objective the deconstruction of all figures of absolute authority, Sigmund Freud included. However frequently Freud, in writing, in his personal life, or in his career as an institution builder, may have seemed devoted to setting himself on the primal father's throne, day to day there was a whole other dimension to Freud's work. What Freud did almost every morning and afternoon was to allow people to cultivate an inflated image of who and what he was, and then guide them in the process of dismantling that image. Over and over again, Freud showed his patients how to draw the gigantic figures in their own past down to size, and they learned this in no other way than by learning to draw Freud himself in more modest, human contours. Freud the sometimes patriarch didn't just develop theories about the destructive effects of patriarchy; he developed a form of teaching that gave people the chance to undo oppressive authority.

Shortly after Max Schur returned from New York, Freud had an attack of "cardiac asthma," and Schur rescued Freud, who by this point did not entirely care to be rescued. Freud now, as it were, forgave Schur for abandoning him, forgave his trip to America, and the old unequal friendship of the great man to his trusted retainer, Lear to Kent, was restored. "During August," Schur recalls, "everything went down hill rapidly. There could be no doubt about an extended recurrence with ulceration. The discoloration of the cheek became more and more marked, indicating the development of a skin necrosis." The odor that came from Freud, Schur says, got worse and worse and was soon impossible to control. It was the stench of Freud's jawbone, rotting away from the cancer. In time, the skin over Freud's cheek became gangrenous. A hole formed, creating what Schur called "open communication between the oral cavity and the outside." The odor became stronger, and flies gathered, so Freud's bed in the study needed to be covered by netting to keep them away. Freud's study, as Schur says, became his sick bay, and he could do nothing but lie there, looking out into his garden.

But the great problem was with Lün, Freud's chow, who had been released from quarantine. The dog had always adored her master. Freud had petted her, walked her, and frequently, too, talked with her: she sometimes seemed to him the sanest presence in his life. But now she cowered on the far side of the sick room because of the smell of decomposition coming from her master.

Freud said that dogs lived fully and even at times joyously because they did not suffer the fundamental human curse of ambivalence. Dogs did not love and hate the same object. They fawned on their masters and snapped at their enemies. They were, to Freud of course, what human beings could never be: creatures who attained a blameless purity of feeling. Freud did not wish to consider the palpable truth that, like humans, dogs are creatures of nature that have undergone domestication and so both love and hate the restrictive world where they find themselves. Freud's idealizations—his intoxications—were few, though he did, it is true, once remark that the only pure love that could exist in the world was the love between a mother and her son: strange news coming from the theorist of the Oedipal complex. But on the matter of dogs, Freud was consistently starry-eyed. He could imagine pure love flowing from his dogs to him—and maybe sometimes from himself back to them. Now this pleasure too was gone. Freud's life was becoming, what he called it in a letter to Princess Bonaparte, "a small island of pain floating on an ocean of indifference."

At the end of the first week of August, the week when Freud surrendered his practice, he also saw the last of the princess—he lost her too. Freud had, in a certain sense, saved the princess's life years ago. It was not that her analysis with him was so successful; at best it had been partially complete. (Though as Freud was never tired of observing, to ask for too much in these endeavors can be foolhardy: in therapy the better is often the enemy of the good.) No, what mattered was that Freud had discerned the princess's energy and good-heartedness, and had seen her intellectual promise as well. He helped her to become an analyst, and he encouraged her to begin writing psycho-analytic studies, which she did with no little success. (Despite Freud's much-publicized skepticism about women's intellectual powers, he could be a potent supporter of women who wanted to develop their minds.) What Freud helped to save the princess from was a life of high-society intrigues, futile love affairs, tourism, and relentless self-absorption.

Then, later in life, Princess Bonaparte helped to save Freud. All the qualities that she developed in her long friendship with him and her association with his strange art—her vitality, confidence, intelligence, bravery—came to bear during the struggle to get Freud out of Vienna. An unusual fairy tale played itself out there: the beautiful rich princess, not the questing knight, arrived to rescue the aged monarch and conduct him out of the Wasteland to a greener, more fertile place. And now the princess was leaving and Freud surely understood that the odds were he would not see her again. For someone as pugnacious as Freud could be—as willing to take offense, as ready to quarrel—he had an extraordinary power to make and to keep friends. People were fond of him. They liked his candor, the vigor of his mind; they liked his humor, which, though it grew darker as time passed, never quite disappeared. Freud had many admirers and disciples and many friends too, but he probably never had a better friend than Marie Bonaparte, who now departed, but who, for the rest of her life—she died in

1962—would be a fierce proponent of the Professor and his cause.

Much of Freud's family was lost to him too. Every day he certainly spent at least some time thinking about his four sisters, for whom he and the princess had been unable to secure visas. They stayed back in Austria, well funded, and with the princess doing all that she could to protect them. Originally there had been five of them in Vienna: Anna, Adolphine, Mitzi, Pauli, and Rosa. Anna, the oldest of the girls, married a brother of Freud's wife, a man named Eli Bernays. She died in New York City on March 11, 1955, at ninety-seven years old.

Adolphine, or Dolfi as she was called, was the only one who never married; she spent most of her life taking care of Freud's mother, Amalia. People thought of her as, in Martin Freud's words, a "rather silly old maid." But Martin tells a story about walking one day in Vienna with his aunt and passing an ordinary-looking middle-class man. Martin did not hear him say anything, but when he had passed, Dolfi exclaimed, "Did you hear what that man said? He called me a dirty stinking Jewess and said it was time we were all killed." At the time, Martin recalls, many of his friends were gentiles—lawyers, doctors, professors. "It seems strange," he says, "that while none of us . . . had any idea of the tragedy which would destroy the children of the Jewish race, a lovable but rather silly old maid foresaw . . . that future."

Dolfi was starved to death in the Jewish ghetto at Theresienstadt; she died on September 29, 1942. The other three sisters were transported from Vienna to Theresienstadt and from there to the concentration camp at Treblinka. They died, murdered by the Nazis, in 1942.

During that September, Freud also lost something along with the rest of the world: that was peace. Three weeks after Freud disbanded his practice, Russia, which Winston Churchill had called "a riddle wrapped in a mystery inside an enigma," became considerably less mystifying. Russia came to terms with Germany and signed a mutual nonaggression pact. Hitler had been declaring communism a mortal enemy from long before the day he came to power in 1933; and Stalin felt little better about Nazism. Yet shortly after the signing, Stalin proposed a toast to the former street rat: "I know how much the German nation loves its Führer," Stalin intoned, "I should therefore like to drink his health."

Hitler ordered that photographs be taken of Stalin at the signing, partly because the führer was curious to know whether Stalin's earlobes were "ingrown and Jewish," as he feared, or "separate and Aryan." The pictures quelled Hitler's anxiety: one shot in particular, a profile, affirmed that Stalin's earlobes were indeed of the non-Jewish variety. Stalin's smoking did, however, concern the führer: in every photograph of Stalin reviewing the treaty and signing it, a cigarette dangled from his mouth. "The signing of the pact is a solemn act that one does not approach with a cigarette in one's lips," Hitler, the lifelong antismoking evangelist, said. (He offered a gold watch to any member of his inner circle who quit tobacco.) Hitler told the photographer to paint out Stalin's cigarettes before releasing the pictures to the press.

Churchill claimed that it was an open question whether Hitler or Stalin loathed the nonaggression pact more. The intrinsic opposition of the two systems was, Churchill believed, unalterable. But Freud's work points to a different interpretation. The distinct economic dispensations, and the diverse iconographies and liturgies of Russian Communism and German Nazism make less difference than one might imagine. These were both governments of the patriarch, appealing to the same perverse and all-too-human desire. The fact that Hitler and Stalin would eventually go to war suggests that under the sun there can only be one genuine man-god; this is so because the contenders for the prize wish it to be and because humanity, alas, often seconds their wish.

The way was open now for Hitler's next move. On September 1, a day when Freud lay in his study, doing what he could to control the pain in his jaw, Nazi troops burst across the border into Poland. The Poles fought back ferociously; sometimes to the last soldier. When the Nazi Panzer divisions came on, Polish cavalrymen charged them with lances set, to predictable effect. Soon the nation would be overrun by the Germans. Hitler took himself up very near to the front to be close to the soldiers: "Front line troops must be assured that the officers share their privations," he said. Every day he was out among the army, riding in his open-topped car when the weather permitted, flourishing his oxhide whip. He took a particular interest in all aspects of the fighting men's lives, particularly their diets. When Hitler's staff suggested that he might go and meet the first trainload of wounded German soldiers, Hitler said that he could not: the sight of their suffering would be too much for him to bear.

Not much later it occured to Hitler that it would be a good idea to eliminate all Polish people from the earth's face and, with the help of many other Germans, he would set to work. But now Hitler simply savored his amazing victory. On the day of the invasion, Britain had sent Hitler yet another of its ultimatums, which he duly ignored. Two days later, both France and England declared war and the conflagration began. The last words that Freud wrote in his journal, a week before the Polish onslaught, were "war panic." Whatever hopes Freud might have had for a tranquil solution to the world's crises were now also lost. When Schur asked Freud if he thought that this would be the last of all wars, Freud answered simply, "My last war."

To Freud's way of thinking, there would probably never be an end to war. He believed that human beings carried a potent charge of aggressive energy and that in the deployment of this energy they generally had only a pair of choices. They could allow their aggressive libido to stay bottled up within, un-discharged. That energy, Freud believed, would frequently become the property of the superego, which would use it to punish the individual, perpetually enhancing his sense of guilt. But there was a salient way out of this dilemma. The individual could aim the force outside, turning it against the world at large. The more passionately he did so, the more fully he would purge himself of inner tensions. Violence opens the blocked spirit, Freud said. But it also creates horrible destruction. Human history, from the Freudian point of view, moves between anxious periods when culture inhibits the destructive drive and periods when the drive can turn outward, in murder, rape, and conquest.

The alternative that Freud offered was for human beings to initiate themselves into the arts of sublimation. It was possible, Freud believed, to convert instinctual energy into energy for science, commerce, and artistic creation. But it was not at all clear how many people would ever be able to manage such a conversion. Freud thought that most people not only lack the capacity to rechannel their instincts, but also lack the ability in art or intellectual pursuits that would make such rechanneling pay off. During Freud's lifetime the world had propelled itself into two world wars, two great upsurges of destruction. This was so for many reasons, Freud suggests in his essay "Why War?" but most saliently because for the great majority of people, it is simply too hard to live with the anxiety and with the relatively attenuated satisfactions that peace can bring. Peace is not only tedious; it causes ongoing suffering, because during peacetime, even the human beings most adept at sublimation deny their fundamental nature. Freud did not believe that much of any civilization could give the majority of its citizens the same measure of satisfaction that acting on instinct could give, and so the chances for an end to war were virtually nonexistent.

In his later work, Freud speaks of something called the Death Drive, by which he means the drive of an organism—human or animal, complex or one-celled—to seek its own destruction. And yet, Freud insists, the organism seeks such destruction exclusively "after its own fashion." The Death Drive, Freud indicates in "Why War?" is the direct result of too much acquiescence to the demands of civilization; it is the result of the steady augmenting of tensions and a corresponding inability to find sufficiently intense pleasure or rewarding work in peaceful civilization. As Freud observes in *Civilization and Its Discontents*, "An artist's joy in creating, in giving his phantasies body, or a scientist's in solving problems or discovering truths, has a special quality. . . . At present we can only say figuratively that such satisfactions seem 'finer and higher.' But their intensity is mild compared with that derived from the sating of crude and primary instinctual impulses; it does not convulse our physical being. And the weak point of this method is that it is not applicable generally: it is accessible to only a few people." In general, to read a book or to write one is no substitute for burning down a library—or at least to doing so in the interest of one noble cause or another.

Arrayed against death is the power that Freud called Eros, which is the force that draws human beings together in large, civilized, and civilizing groups. Yet as Freud understood, humanity can turn collectively against Eros, turn collectively against love's pleasures, and affirm death exclusively. "Long live death!" the Spanish fascists used to chant; Freud would have had no trouble understanding why.

It is odd, but one of the final losses, and in a sense the loss that Freud found to be least bearable, was a very simple one. At a certain point late in his illness, Freud became too weak to read. Freud said once that he invented psychoanalysis because it had no literature—that is, psychoanalysis had no official body of scholarly texts that one had to master to enter the field. What that meant was that Freud could read as he liked. And this he did, constantly. Freud read a small library's worth of archaeology; he read extensively in anthropology for *Totem and Taboo*; he read Twain and Heine, Goethe and Schiller; he read Shakespeare in English, drawing one idea after another from the plays; he read Milton's *Paradise Lost*, calling it one of his favorite books. He liked Kipling, Zola, Anatole France, and Macaulay. He might have found time to read a scientific treatise or two and perhaps, despite his protests, a work of non-psychoanalytical psychology as well. Freud read because he wanted to know about every significant kind of human behavior, collective and individual, past and present; he wanted to experience every kind of art that had moved people.

The last book Freud was able to read is a variation on the Faust myth, Balzac's *La peau de chagrin* (*The wild ass's skin*). In it, the protagonist, Raphael de Valentin, acquires a wild donkey's skin that he can use to grant all of his wishes. But in Balzac's cosmos, as in Freud's, there are no consequential pleasures that go unpaid for: nothing is got for nothing. Each time Raphael makes a wish, the skin shrinks. When the skin dissolves completely, he is given to know, his life will end. Raphael starts out by wishing for the kinds of things that his creator was known to pine after, and that Freud himself believed motivated most passionate, worldly men: fame, wealth, and the love of beautiful women. Near the opening of the book, there is a drunken, debauched orgy scene of the sort that only Balzac can write. Raphael gets everything that he's been hoping for there and later, but the price is exorbitant. With every granted wish, not only does the wild ass's skin diminish, but Raphael loses more of his vigor until, in time, he becomes a waning, withered medical curiosity, poked at, prodded, and condescended to by a troupe of the most distinguished physicians in Paris. What makes it the more plangent—in Balzac anything plangent must be made more so—is that Raphael has finally found true love, in the glowing form of Pauline, once his impoverished neighbor in the rooming house her mother owns, and later a stupendously rich but still innocent girl.

How could Freud have borne such a book? In it, Raphael enjoys all the worldly pleasures, from sensual indulgence to intellectual creation. (In his lonely room before he gets rich, he composes what sounds like a Schopenhauerian book on the subject of the will.) Raphael lives in Balzac's charged world, where everything is preternaturally heightened: the kitchen maids have regal beauty, the stable boys are geniuses in the making, the silver at dinner shines like the moon, and the mud on the road is a foot deep and reeks of the graveyard. In reading the novel, Freud surely did not see his own life pass before his eyes: the strange mixture of adventure and quiet, daring and restraint, combined to feed Freud's singular genius is not readily to be found in Balzac's fiction. But Freud did see *a* life pass before him, and a vitally intense one at that. How, reading this volume, could Freud at least not sometimes have pined for some remission from his illness? How could he not have begged life for a second chance?

Then there is the manner of Raphael's dying. As he makes more wishes, often against his conscious intentions—the book chronicles what Freud would have seen as the war between the hungry id and the often-baffled ego—the magic skin shrinks and Raphael's health declines. He ends up in a sanitarium, where the other patients despise him, and gradually, horribly, he wastes away. "This was the proper book for me to read," Freud told Max Schur when he had finished with it. "It deals with shrinking and starvation." Freud, as Schur remarked, could look on Raphael's panic in the end, as he too shrunk to nothingness, and resolve to do better. He could resolve to die with quiet dignity, rather than to succumb to terror. Whatever inner use he made of the book, after he finished it, there was to be no more reading: Freud had to face what he was going to face without the consolation of books, sacred or profane.

On September 19, Ernest Jones, Freud's most loyal retainer, came to the house at Maresfield Gardens to see Freud and, Jones believed, to say good-bye. When Jones arrived, Freud was unconscious, lying on the couch, beneath the mosquito netting. "I . . . called him by name as he dozed," Jones recalled. "He opened his eyes, recognized me and waved his hand, then dropped it with a highly expressive gesture." To Jones that gesture conveyed "a wealth of meaning: greetings, farewell, resignation. It said as plainly as possible, 'The rest is silence.'"

On September 21, Max Schur sat at Freud's bedside, looking at the wasted old man, with his decaying, foul-smelling jaw. It must have been difficult for Schur to believe that here before him was perhaps the most potent and influential intellect of his century, the man who had probably done more than any other to change the way people in the West thought about who and what they were. Now Freud simply looked cadaverous: he was pale and brittle and weighed next to nothing. But Freud still had some strength of will in him. He took his doctor's hand and said, "My dear Schur, you certainly remember our first talk. You promised me then not to forsake me when the time comes. Now it is nothing but torture and makes no sense anymore."

Schur let Freud know that he had not forgotten the promise he made. "Ich danke Ihnen," Freud said. "I thank you." He told Schur to "talk it over with Anna, and if she thinks it's right, make an end of it." Schur spoke to Anna and Anna sorrowfully concurred with her father's wish.

That same day, Schur gave Freud an injection of three centigrams of morphine, a dose much stronger than he would have used if the objective had only been to relieve pain. Schur was now assisting in a suicide. He gave Freud another injection that day, then a third on September 22. Freud lapsed into a coma, but he held on to life. Midnight came and on Saturday, September 23, Sigmund Freud was still alive.

That day was Yom Kippur, the Jewish Day of Atonement, and in the morning many Jews in London would be making their way to synagogue, continuing the ritual of prayer and fasting begun the night before, entreating the God whom Sigmund Freud had done all he could to do away with for forgiveness. All through London now, there were sandbags in place, in preparation for the air raids, which would begin soon and at horrible cost. Red pillar boxes had been marked with yellow detector tape to test for poison gas and people carried gas masks with them as they did their daily business. All through the city, statues were being removed or enclosed in brick for protection. British war planes flew over London, frightening dogs and cats with their eerie drone. Overhead floated barrage balloons, enormous airships supposedly strong enough to destroy any aircraft that collided with them. In the London parks, there were no more deck chairs for concert-goers, for fear that the chairs would block access to the recently dug trenches. (Rumors were spreading that the trenches were to be used as burial sites after the inevitable slaughter the air raids would cause.) Soon the great statue of Eros would be gone from Piccadilly Circus to protect it from bombs. Eros's antagonist in Freud's mythology, the force he simply called Death, was ready to ascend.

At three in the morning on Saturday, September 23, 1939, Sigmund Freud died from cancer and from Schur's morphine overdoses.

Many years before, Freud had divulged a wish about the way that he hoped to die. He wanted, he said, never to have to live without his mental capacities intact. He feared nothing so much as a stroke, paralysis not only of the body, but more disturbingly, of the mind. Freud declared that he wanted to "die in harness." Writing to his friend Oskar Pfister, he put it this way: "With all the resignation before destiny that suits an honest man, I have one wholly secret entreaty: only no invalidism, no paralysis of one's powers through bodily mis-

ery. Let us die in harness, as King Macbeth says." Freud
wanted to go down doing his work, with his sword—his
intellect—still flashing.

And Freud did that, or very nearly so. The weeks leading up
to his major decline in August were trying for him because,
though he could read and think with some clarity, he did not
have the strength to write. Perhaps for a while he thought that
the power to write—to put his imprint on the world—might
return. But when he saw that it would not, he knew he had to
make an end of it. Freud, the longtime atheist, never called out
on God; he never asked celestial forgiveness; he never recanted
his lack of faith: he was a stubbornly secular man to the end.
When he was sick and dying, he stuck to his arduously created
views and values, affirming what he had in other, better days.
Freud was true to himself through to the end.

Freud particularly relished a story that goes something like
this: An atheist, who has sold insurance for a living, lies on his
deathbed. There comes to visit him in his hour of need a
minister determined to save the poor man's soul. The minister
spends two hours, then three sitting with the man, grappling
with Satan, or whatever force it is that stands between salvation
and the wayward salesman. When the minister finally leaves the
sickroom, all the man's friends crowd around. Is he saved? Is his
soul pure? No, no, the minister has to admit, all his entreaties
failed. But the minister is happy to announce that he's now the
owner of a new insurance policy acquired at a splendid dis-
count.

What touched Freud in the tale, no doubt, was that salesman's cheerful defiance; he possessed an admirable share of

what Emerson liked to call "good-humored inflexibility." As to Freud, he was more than capable of such inflexibility until the end of his life, as his determination to publish the Moses book dramatized well enough. When the social superego smiled on Freud in London, he nodded in gratitude, but worked on in his own way, and finally gave the world *Moses and Monotheism*, when what it wanted from him was something far more conforming and tame. In Vienna, he had, in the words of the Puritan poem he so much admired, fallen "on evil days . . . / In darkness and with dangers compassed round." Yet the old man stayed firm and brave; he even had the equanimity to produce a flourish of wit from time to time.

Freud died without religious or metaphysical consolation. For the past two thousand years, the great majority of people in the West have died with hope for an afterlife intact. Freud left the world as a believer in one thing only—in the future promise human beings might have to know themselves a little more (which sometimes meant simply knowing how ignorant they could be about themselves) and because of such knowledge to live better than they would have. Freud left the world with a certain composure, for he had done his work. He had reached that point aptly described by Nietzsche: "The most fortunate author," he says, "is one who is able to say as an old man that all he had of life-giving, invigorating, uplifting, enlightening thoughts and feelings still lives on in his writings, and that he himself is only the gray ash, while the fire has been rescued and carried forth everywhere."

An institution, Emerson says, is the lengthened shadow of a single individual, and of no institution and no individual could this be truer than of psychoanalysis and of its founder, Freud. By dying as he did, Freud increased the length and breadth of the authoritative shadow that he would cast forward into time. He died in a way that would enhance his reputation as a leader, that would engender people's loyalty over the years, that would move them in the way that kings' and potentates' passing can do, move them with the majestic sense that here was a man who was more than a man. This was someone worth believing in with fervor and worth following into the future. Freud wanted to create belief and adherence down through the time, and—though it is not entirely tasteful to say as much—he arranged his death in such a way as to help him to do exactly that.

Pondering the death of Sigmund Freud, one thinks of the lines Auden wrote about him in the great elegy, about how "the autocratic pose, / The paternal strictness he distrusted, still / Clung to his utterance and features." Auden's lines apply to all of Freud's career, but have an especial bearing on the hour of his death. There was, perhaps, something too decorous, too stoic, too managed about it, at least when one considers the kinds of things that Freud, overall, stood for. Freud had his agreement with the younger retainer, Schur, a man who admired and even adored Freud; he had Anna to do his bidding; he had his reconstructed study, which he'd loaded with his books and treasures, like a pharaoh surrounding himself with his possessions for transport into the next world; he had his memorable farewell utterance: "Now it is nothing but torture and makes no sense anymore."

Consider, by contrast, some other parting words. Oscar

Wilde, mortally ill in a Paris flophouse, announced, "I am in a duel to death with this wallpaper. One of us has to go." Goethe cried out, enigmatically, movingly, "More light!" John Maynard Keynes, looking back on a life that was not without its pleasures, said, "I wish that I had drunk more champagne." Standing on the scaffold, about to die, Sir Walter Raleigh proclaimed, "This is a sharp medicine, but a sure remedy for all evils." Picasso petitioned all and sundry to drink to him. P. T. Barnum, American to the last, as Freud would see it, inquired into that day's circus receipts from Madison Square Garden. At his own end, Freud was sober and correct: "Now it is nothing but torture."

Freud had spent the past twenty fertile years deconstructing the human need to submit to figures of absolute authority. No one knew more about the subtle intricacies of power than did he. Yet the "autocratic pose" did indeed cling to him. It is not surprising that it did. Freud believed that he had unlocked the secret of power: he saw why people reduced themselves to quivering submission before a certain kind of greatness. And all through his life, he was tempted to take on the great man's role. When he did, the world was more likely to listen, more likely to believe. Freud was a speculative genius, but also an institution builder, and for the institution called psychoanalysis to last, Freud occasionally felt impelled to trade on some of the tactics of domination that psychoanalysis existed to undermine. With his death, Freud contributed to an image of himself and of his work that is at some variance with the best of what psychoanalysis teaches. As Adam Phillips suggests in a brilliant essay on Freud's last days, Freud died as an authority, writ large, yet he wrote and often lived as someone who asked humanity to turn away from all large-scale coercive powers. Freud's death concentrates the ultimate riddle of Sigmund Freud: he was the great cultural patriarch, who stood for nothing so much as for the dismantling of patriarchy.

If one looks at the Moses book a little more patiently than its first reviewers were in a position to do, another dimension of Freud comes to the fore, one that enriches and complicates the image of the authoritative Sigmund Freud. *Moses and Monotheism* may take off from the fierce critique of religion, monotheism in particular, that goes back to *Future of an Illusion*. But the book, despite the denunciations from the pious it received, is better disposed toward faith, and toward Judaism in particular, than any of Freud's prior work. To Freud, the essence of Judaism, whether it originated with the Jews or the Egyptians, lies in its adherents' ability to believe in an invisible god. The Jew is the one who can invest himself in what is not present, for God exists in the mind of the Jew and there alone. This salient fact distinguishes Judaism from the desert faiths it developed near and competed with. No matter who may have conceived of monotheism first, the Jews were the ones who were able to sustain it. Surely the Jews always threatened to slide back into idol worship, as they did when they danced around the golden calf while Moses was on Sinai receiving the Laws. For the Jews, like everyone else, deeply desired *to see* divinity.

The pleasures of sight, Freud insists, are intense, nearly instinctive pleasures. Human beings revel in appearance: they delight in the many-toned glories of the world. To renounce the visible in the interest of the unseen is an enormously difficult human task. An intense satisfaction is then replaced by a satisfaction that is less vital, less intense, but more valuable in the long run. "Among the precepts of the Mosaic religion," Freud says, "there is one that is of greater importance than appears to begin with. This is the prohibition against making an image of God—the compulsion to worship a God whom one cannot see. . . . If this prohibition were accepted, it must have a profound effect. For it meant that a sensory perception was given second place to what may be called an abstract idea—a triumph of intellectuality over sensuality or, strictly speaking, an instinctual renunciation, with all its necessary psychological consequences."

When Salvador Dalí came to visit, Freud remarked to him rather enigmatically that "Moses is flesh of sublimation." What he meant, it seems, is that Moses was the man who had fully absorbed the imperative to accept the abstract god. He had surrendered more direct, more instinctual satisfactions for the civilized and civilizing satisfactions of believing in a sole, unseen deity. Yet sublimation hurts. It means subordinating one aspect of the psyche, the id, to others, the ego and superego. But the id does not easily remain in a subordinate position. Sublimation creates inner tension, creates pain. Moses presumably suffered from the effort of continuing to believe in an invisible god when so many other tantalizing religious illusions were available. Similarly, Moses suffered when (at least in Freud's interpretation) he compelled himself to sublimate his anger at the reveling Jews who betrayed Yahweh while Moses was on the mountain. Moses was someone capable of more inner tension, more inner conflict than others: he could want and not want something at the same time, feel both desire and its antithesis, and live in that state for prolonged periods. Freud suggests that the ability to sustain such tension tuned to a high degree is what makes someone a hero of civilization. The great swordsman Achilles or one of his many, many descendents can allow all his energies to move in one direction, toward glory. But sword law is not civilization. Ambivalence that has been fully assimilated, that has infused the flesh as well as the mind and spirit, is what civilization is about for Freud, and in this regard Moses was heroic, and heroic in a new way.

In *Moses and Monotheism*, Freud argues that taking God into the mind enriches the individual immeasurably. The ability to internalize an invisible god vastly enhances people's capacity for abstraction. If they can worship what is not there, they can also reflect on what is not there, or on what is presented to them in symbolic, not immediate, terms. So the mental labor of monotheism prepares the Jews to distinguish themselves in mathematics, in law, in science, and in literary art—in all the activities, in other words, that involve making an abstract model of experience, in words or numbers or lines, and working with the abstraction to achieve control over nature or to bring humane order to life.

Freud calls this internalizing process an "advance in intellectuality," and it makes its practitioners not only more adept at certain activities, but also rather proud. The ability to renounce a deep satisfaction always results in pain for the individual, but because the over-I approves of that pain and the renunciation that causes it, the individual is likely to develop an exalted sense of himself. He becomes proud about what he has achieved through sublimation and he looks down on those who cannot effect the same feat. "Moses," Freud says, "conveyed to the Jews an exalted sense of being a chosen people. The dematerialization of God brought a fresh and valuable contribution to their secret treasure." The hero of sublimation is anxious, yes, but his anxiety comes in the service of higher ideals; if he is a martyr, he is a martyr to civilization, and that is something to be proud of.

So according to Freud, Judaism has made a grand contribution to collective life. But that contribution is not enough: Judaism is still a form of monotheism, and accordingly, an infantilizing system of belief. Freud's implication is that humanity needs to take another step on the road of inwardness and abstraction. For belief in the invisible God might prepare the ground not only for science and literature and law, but also for belief in that internal, unseen structure that Freud calls the psyche. Someone who can contemplate an invisible God, Freud suggests, is in a much better position to take seriously the invisible, but perhaps determining, dynamics of the inner world. To live well, to begin to know himself, the modern individual, with his divided psyche, must live with abstraction. This Judaism, with its commitment to one unseen God, opens the way for doing. But it is psychoanalysis that truly makes such introspection possible, offering the terms—ego and id and superego and all the rest—that allow individuals to begin to know their mysterious inner lives.

This gift of inwardness, Freud suggests, is a gift of Judaism, and not of Christianity. Christianity began by taking a cultural step backward in the direction of pagan idolatry. Christianity diluted Judaism's insistence on the invisible—and so compromised its intellectual bequest—by resurrecting the whole panoply of pagan gods. The old idols came back as the Christian saints; the old temples returned as Catholic churches full of color, pomp, scent, and sound. Christianity, despite Protestant urges to fight idolatry, was still, to Freud, essentially a throwback to the old religions. (The Protestants, however severe, still believed in a God who had walked the earth.) Judaic abstraction led to the true development of the mind. In Freud's revised way of thinking, God is still a figure to displace, but belief in him is a necessary stage on the way to far better belief.

Fascism, Freud would have noticed, is emphatically eye-intense. Fascism gives pageantry, color, light, and noise to people who suffer from the kind of privation that Judaism brought to the world and that influenced Protestantism, especially puritanical Protestantism, as well as Islam. Freud speculates, questionably but shrewdly, that one of the causes of anti-Semitism might be Christian rage at the instinctual satisfactions that the Jews have taken away. The Jews effected the great renunciation. The Jews were the ones who would not believe that the gods walked the earth and could be seen among mankind. Humanity wants those old gods back, wants the pagan grandeur, and in fascist pageantry, humanity gets something of the miracle and mystery and authority that it craves. There is no social ceremony more antithetical to Judaic and psychoanalytic inwardness than the mass rally, where the torches flare, the searchlights play against the sky, the banners float and snap in the wind, and the leader reveals the truth behind all appearances.

Moses and Monotheism suggests a genealogy of culture that runs from paganism to the Jewish faith, as exemplified by Moses, then on to the highly secular faith that is psychoanalysis. In this genealogy, Freud becomes a second Moses, leading his small band out into the wilderness, beset and troubled, but confident that in the long run the Western world will adapt to the ethos of psychoanalysis, much as it has to the belief in one invisible god. All through his life, Freud resisted the idea that psychoanalysis could be what its detractors liked to say it was, a Jewish science. But at the end of his career, he implicitly joined his way of thought to the Jewish tradition, and joined his own sense of self to his image of the paragon of Judaism, Moses.

The identification with Moses has another, perhaps more consequential dimension to Freud. For by brooding on Moses, Freud comes to see what kind of hero he himself aspires to be. In Moses, Freud sees a new kind of authority. Up until this point, Freud's reflections on authority have ended up at the same place. Authority is inevitably male, narcissistic, overbearing, self-interested, arbitrary, and, quite often, tyrannical. Yet in Moses, Freud often (though not always) sees something different. Moses can project all the patriarchal qualities, true. But Moses is distinct from other sorts of leaders in that he is a hero of sublimation: he is a divided being who achieves his authority not by being self-willed and appetitive, but by intelligently rechanneling his impulses and teaching others to do the same. He renounces the pagan gods; he gives laws that rest on prohibition; when the Jews rebel, Freud argues in his early essay on the prophet, Moses succeeds in restraining himself from raging against them. Freud's Moses, unlike the archetypal leader, lives with inner conflict and anxiety, and he does so in the interest of civilization. What Moses surely suggests to Freud—and should suggest to us—is that it may be possible to be an authority, to have an influence, without being a conventional patriarch.

The fascist leader, who embodies the general will, sees what he wants and takes it; desires this or that, and moves when the time is right. He has no internal conflicts, at least as the world apprehends it: he wants what he wants. The hero of civilization, on the other hand, knows how to restrain his immediate desire in the interest of something better. He knows how to live with the anxiety that conflicting and unresolved wishes bring and he takes this anxiety as a condition of life, rather than as something for which he needs to find a personal or cultural remedy. Perhaps he is never terribly happy, but his self-aware restraint is appealing to others—it gives them new powers in science and art and government; it makes them proud of themselves, because they have been able to perform a piece of instinctual renunciation. Unlike the fascist leader, Freud's leader is capable of signifying his self-division: he can be ironic; he's not averse to making a joke. (Both ironic speech and joking, Freud indicates, show awareness that there is more than one simple reality to take into account, one truth: they testify to there being contending forces at play in the world, contending interpretations of experience.) And too, the civilized leader's example of restraint and circumspection stops people from devouring

one another, which on a certain level is what they most wish to
do.

Freud saw that the human relation to authority would
always be ambivalent: it would involve both love and hate. We
adore the primal father for his capacity to provide unity,
purpose, assurance, and truth. But in time we can come to
detest him too. For we see that his pure truth is too simple to
be effective, that his unity is too painful to sustain, and that he
suspends too many human freedoms. Then we turn against
him furiously. Freud can at times look like a dictator of the
cultural realm; so it is to be expected that his reputation will
go through the oddest and most apparently inexplicable turns
and twists. Now he is up, now he is down, for reasons that are
rather unreasonable. But of course Freud is different from
other patriarchs in politics and culture in that he is constantly
teaching us how much we need to debunk patriarchy and
giving us the conceptual tools to do so. (Hitler, after all, did
not come on with a program to end all Hitlers.) The fact that
Freud is both patriarch and anti-patriarch makes his cultural
presence all the more difficult to assimilate and causes many
strange perturbations in the way the world conceives of him.
Those perturbations genuinely matter when they divide us
from what is best in Freud's thinking.

Freud, one might say, triggered a large-scale transference in
the mind of the West. That is, people have aimed at him all the
hopes and hatreds that have in the past infused their relations to
authority. Accordingly, Freud inspires what he would call "an
artificial illness," in which the regressive dynamics of authority
are made visible and susceptible to analysis. All of the best that

Freud offers—his ideas about dreams and jokes and the structure of the psyche, his suggestion that there is more to know and less to judge than we had imagined possible—all of this legacy at times disappears. In its place, we have Freud the cocaine user, Freud the misogynist, Freud the ersatz scientist. Perhaps this phase will pass and Freud will become a mortal god, a cultural patriarch, again; but really that is very little better.

The West can, and perhaps in time it will, use analysis to stop repeating its strange relation to Freud (which he of course in many ways brought on himself) and finally work it through. The objective of such analysis isn't to dismiss or debunk Freud, but to be able to read his work with irony, humor, detachment, and due openness when what he has to say proves to be illuminating—as it so often is.

In his later period, Sigmund Freud predicted two shocking phenomena of the twentieth and twenty-first centuries. The first was the rise of tyranny. The revolutions of the eighteenth and nineteenth centuries, in the United States, in France, all through Latin America, and elsewhere, persuaded many people that an age of democratic liberalism had begun. Monarchy and aristocracy seemed to be waning everywhere. Walt Whitman was in many ways representative when he prophesied the rise of the common man, the widening of the franchise, the freeing of slaves, majority rule. But it turned out that people did not always want freedom or equality; they found democracy ineffectual, unglamorous, and disorienting. It fomented confusion inside the self and out. Human beings dreamed of order, and lo there stepped forward all the figures of destiny glad to offer purpose, resolution, and Truth. If this tendency began in the twentieth century with Lenin, Franco, Mussolini, and Hitler, then continued on through Stalin and Mao, it surely has not come to an end. It sometimes appears that in the twentieth century and the twenty-first, human beings have been engaged in counterevolution. They have turned back to more primitive states of mind and of government. Freud offers some strong hypotheses about why this should be so: he begins to account for humanity's revolt against its own better interests.

Freud's work also predicts the new birth of the fundamentalist urge. Religion in the twentieth and twenty-first centuries did not become more private, more provisional, more nuanced—at least not for many. And it did not disappear—far from it. Rather, the centuries have seen the rise of ferociously patriarchal religions, not only in Islam, but in the Christian world as well. The most powerful and most technologically advanced nation in the twenty-first century has a sizable constituency who wish for little so much as religious rule by the state, theocracy.

From the Freudian perspective, authoritarian religion and authoritarian politics are two sides of one debased coin. They feed off each other, borrow techniques, modes of persuasion, and iconography. They traffic in the same sorts of miracle, mystery, and authority. And they are the most plausible form of human destiny: they are where humanity will go without potent efforts of resistance. Freud's work suggests that no one should ever think that fascism and fundamentalism are gone and done with. There is no such thing as an eternal triumph over them. Because they are so integral to what it is to be human, no one should even think that humanity has defeated them once and for all. This was the error of the liberal nineteenth century.

Freud also warns against thinking that the fascist and the fundamentalist are radically other. Book after book, essay after essay, has come into the world trying to show what set the German Nazis apart from everyone else. It was their political past, their culture, their military tradition; it was the debased Treaty of Versailles; it was the Depression of 1929. The same scholarly ritual is visited on Japan and, to a lesser extent, on Italy. We seem desperate to know how different these peoples are from ourselves. Freud indicates that such thinking is delusory: we are all fascists, we are all fundamentalists, at least potentially. Through authoritarianism we attain assurance and happiness—though of a certain sort. It is only constant critical labor that keeps the worst political and religious possibilities from becoming fact.

Freud also suggests that fascism and fundamentalism, because of their amazing powers of attraction, will always constitute an emergency. When a powerful or rich nation turns to either, something must be done, and the more quickly, the better. One of the reasons that France and England may have been slow to act prior to the Second World War was that their statesmen did not understand the joy—no less a word should attach to it—that fascism offers people. Inner strife dissolves and the people become powerful and strong. They have never felt so good before and they will not readily give that feeling up. Others see their joy and are drawn to it. Such people make determined and potent foes.

When religious fundamentalism crosses national borders and aligns itself with authoritarian politics, nations that aspire to democracy must deal with an enormous threat. Democracy's foes, then, are exultant with purpose and full of hunger for battle. Their doubts are gone. Democracy's struggle is all the more difficult because its proponents must resist becoming as unified, monolithic, and unquestioning as their foes. They must restrain themselves from becoming fundamentalists who fight for human freedom.

One of the ways that some people attempt to resolve the crisis of authority is to believe in nothing at all—or to pretend to. If one does not invest in any authority, if one is skeptical of everything, then surely one will not succumb to the over-I at its worst. This way of life, which sometimes goes under the name of postmodernism, denies the human hunger for belief entirely. As such, it starves the individual of what he desperately needs— authority in some form—and leaves him all the more open to being appropriated by this or that coercing system when the bad times come, as they will.

To Freud, the self-aware person is continually in the process of deconstructing various god replacements and returning once again to a more skeptical and ironic middle ground. The sane, or relatively sane, self is constantly being duped by this Truth or that (the hunger is very strong; that's simply the way we are) and then coming back to himself and finding more reasonable authorities. He's perpetually consulting his experience, sifting data, questing amid the knowledge of the past and the day-to-day life of the present to find out what is good in the way of belief. He'll ultimately surrender neither to the belief in nothing, nor to the belief in the great One. His life is one of constant self-criticism, and even then he's perpetually surprised at how often he falls for another idol or decides, however wittingly, to give it up and to believe he believes in nothing. But his is also a life of discovery and pleasure at the unexpected, if provisional, truths and fresh possibilities that the world throws his way. He feels, on balance, more than fortunate to be alive. Such people can be quite formidable when they're pushed to the wall. (Fundamentalists and fascists should be warned.) They are accustomed to thinking for themselves and to doing what the moment requires. They are practical and resourceful and they do not always need to wait for orders from on high. They don't freeze up when their leaders disappear or die. They don't need their fathers to be with them all the time.

Acknowledgments

Anyone writing about Freud's life has not one, but two remarkable biographies to acknowledge: Ernest Jones's humane, generous three-volume treatment, *The Life and Work of Sigmund Freud*, and Peter Gay's astonishingly comprehensive and thoughtful *Freud: A Life for Our Time*. A writer treating the last phase of Freud's life has yet a third figure to thank, Michael Molnar, whose editing of *The Diary of Sigmund Freud* is distinguished for its wide range of learning and knowledge of Freud's thought. The secondary literature on Freud is of high quality and I have profited from all of the books listed in the bibliography and more. Still, for the purpose of the current study, two authors stand out. One is the late Philip Rieff, whose *Freud: The Mind of the Moralist* is a model of ethical engagement; the other is Adam Phillips, who in more than a dozen volumes has described and analyzed Freud's thinking—and brought it forward in multiple ways.

This book also profited from generous institutional backing. The John Simon Guggenheim Foundation supported the project, as did the Daniels family and the National Endowment for the Humanities, sponsors of a Distinguished Teaching Professorship at the University of Virginia. (Thanks to Raymond Nelson for working to create the professorship and to Marva Barnett for guiding its deployment.) My deans,

Edward Ayers and Karen Ryan, gave crucial help in speeding this book along, as did the ever-generous chair of the English department, Gordon Braden. To all three, I am extremely grateful. Thanks to my other department chairs as well, Michael Levenson, Jahan Ramazani, and Alison Booth, and to all of my colleagues in the University of Virginia English department. I am grateful also to the University's President, John Casteen, whose conferral of a University Professorship was a great honor and encouragement.

Gillian Blake again gave me the benefit of her brilliant editing, making the book better in a dozen ways. I'm most fortunate to have her as ally and adviser. This is the fourth book of mine that Chris Calhoun has represented. He was involved at every stage, as analyst, negotiator, supporter, and friend—and for all of this I am again grateful. Michael Pollan read this book in draft, as he has all of my books, and made it much better with sharp editorial comments. Yet more important was the gift of his ongoing friendship: his generous encouragement was crucial to my getting the book done. His example as an author who brings challenging ideas to a general audience, and who writes with constant respect for his reader, served as an inspiration throughout. I am grateful, too, to Nick Meyer, not only for helpful comments, but for being exemplary in his effort always to reach the highest possible standard in writing. I also thank Richard Rorty; the benefits of having him as a colleague, a coteacher, friend, and critic have been beyond expression: no writer has given me more by way of example than he has.

For help on matters of history, thanks to Erik Midelfort, Maya Jasanoff, and Alon Confino. For research help, I am indebted to John Havard, Katie Matson, Peter Teigland, Sara Hoover, and Ryan Condell. For exemplary work in the last phase, thanks to Mike O'Connor, Cheryll Lewis, and Ben Adams.

Thanks, too, to my former teachers, D. R. Lenson (sax-man extraordinaire), Doug Meyers (who did a turn as Frank Lears), Alan Cheuse (who understood this project from the beginning), and (from the days of my dissertation on Freud) four marvelous and singular instructors, J. Hillis Miller, Harold Bloom, Geoffrey Hartman, and Leslie Brisman.

Thanks to Alex Star, gifted, generous editor, who gave me a chance to begin developing some of the ideas in this book for the *New York Times* and to Paul H. Fry, whose invitation to speak on Freud helped push the project out of some dense springtime mud. The Philoctetes Society in New York kindly offered me the opportunity to contribute to discussions on Freud as did the sponsors of the conference on Freud's Jewish World, and for those opportunities I am grateful.

My wife Liz showed me how and why this was a consequential project, even when I doubted it, and supported me with her vast generosity throughout the process. She also read the manuscript astutely and made fine suggestions. Matthew, my older son, infused some of his high spirits and zest for living into the writing. My brother, Philip, and my mother, Eileen, took a generous interest in the development of this work, for which I warmly thank them. To Willie, my fellow maker and perpetual inspiration, this book is dedicated.

All errors and slips (Freudian though they may appear) are mine.

Notes

Vienna

For the narrative of Freud's life in Vienna, this section draws particularly on Peter Gay's *Freud: A Life for Our Time*, Ernest Jones's *The Life and Work of Sigmund Freud*, and Michael Molnar's annotations to *The Diary of Sigmund Freud*. For information on Hitler, the chapter makes use of John Toland's *Adolf Hitler* and Ian Kershaw's *Hitler*, as well as of August Kubizek's contemporary account. For the historical events in Germany and in Austria during the late 1930s, the chapter frequently looks to Richard J. Evans's excellent volume *The Third Reich in Power*, as well as eyewitness accounts by William L. Shirer and G. E. R. Gedye.

7   "some incredible daydream": S. Freud, *An Autobiographical Study, Standard Edition*, vol. 20, p. 52. (Henceforth cited as *SE*.)

10   "burning my books": Jones, vol. 3, p. 182.

12   "than any other German": Schuschnigg account, p. 15. For Schuschnigg's version of the meeting, see pp. 3–27.

16   "needed it most": E. Freud, ed., *Letters*, p. 8. (Henceforth cited as *Letters*.)

17   "a homosexual competition": S. Freud, *Civilization and Its Discontents, SE*, vol. 21, p. 90.

20   "Foolish Body decays": Erdman and Bloom, p. 783.

21 "and its ideology": Gedye account, p. 242.

21 "into audible words": Gedye, p. 243.

21 "come into consideration": cited in Molnar, p. 228.

24 "vengeance on the Romans": S. Freud, *The Interpretation of Dreams*, *SE*, vol. 4, p. 197.

25 "afresh with both": S. Freud, *Interpretation of Dreams*, *SE*, vol. 5, p. 483.

25 "in the opposition": *Letters*, p. 367.

26 "not altogether unjust": Jones, vol 1, p. 348.

27 "hour has struck": Clare account, pp. 173–4.

27 "clear and open manner": cited in Toland, p. 466.

28 "the pro-German population": Toland, p. 468.

29 "he was hanged": Churchill, pp. 243–4.

30 "prepared to do": Paskauskas, ed., p. 419.

33 than Sigmund Freud: Gay, p. 454.

34 "God save Austria": Shirer account, p. 99.

35 "Hang Schuschnigg": Gedye account, p. 295.

35 "never, whatever happens": cited in Evans, 651.

36 "both your houses": *Letters*, p. 420.

36 "fall on me": E. Freud, ed., *Letters of Freud and Zweig*, p. 133.

37 "to Rome, like you": Paskauskas, ed., p. 757.

38 "get them so fast": Shirer account, p. 103.

41 "became commonplace everywhere": Gay, p. 590.

42 "holy is profaned": Marx and Engels, p. 223.

44 "estranged from barbarism": McGuire and Hull, eds., p. 194.

45 "the medium of revelation": DeLillo, p. 72.

46 "I am here": Huss, pp. 19–20.

47 "the German Reich": Brook-Shepherd account, p. 201.

47 "Jews killing themselves": Shirer account, p. 110.

48 " 'and start scrubbing' ": Danimann account in Schmidt, ed., pp. 44–5.

48 "weeps all night long": Shirer account, p. 110.

48 " 'Jewish looking fellow' ": Shirer account, p. 109.

51 "in bright daylight": Zweig, p. 405.

53 "I can blame them": Koestler, p. 499.

54 "reinforcement from others": S. Freud, *Group Psychology and the Analysis of the Ego, SE*, vol. 18, p. 123.

54 "check on narcissism": ibid., p. 124.

56 guide his performances: Toland, p. 232.

59 "body marched off": M. Freud, p. 210.

61 "to give up smoking": Pfeiffer, ed., p. 113.

62 "for her later life": *Letters*, p. 440.

71 contained, sublimated anger: S. Freud, "The Moses of Michelangelo," *SE*, vol. 13, pp. 211–38.

72 "for a single visit": Jones, vol. 3, p. 219.

72 "to leave Vienna": cited in Clark, p. 505.

74 "what I mean": Paskauskas, ed., p. 61.

74 "done with life": Jones, vol. 3, p. 219.

77 "I were ruined": cited in Bertin, p. 156. For material on Freud and the princess, see Bertin, pp. 155–7.

78 "upon American opinion": cited by Clark, p. 506.

80 "a shopping expedition": M. Freud, p. 212.

84 "the Hero of Culture": Jones, vol. 3, p. 180.

86 "by personal experience": Ibid., p. 221.

87 "'unkind to the Jews'": Ibid., p. 222.

87 "Amazing March": cited by Molnar, p. 232.

88 "beings also": Friedrich, p. 385.

90 "of my imagination": *Letters*, p. 424.

90 "to the present day": ibid., p. 439.

91 "in my story": H.D., p. 162.

91 "she understood everything": cited in Molnar, p. 214.

92 "this production, too": *Letters*, p. 434.

92 "'Unites us both'": *Letters*, p. 434.

93 "little golden head'": Bonaparte, p. 123.

93 "written the *Iliad*": ibid.

93 "is being translated": *Letters*, p. 437.

96   "your children, Kubizek": Kubizek, p. 280. For an account of the meeting, see Kubizek, pp. 278–281.

96   "joy could say": cited in Weyr, p. 73.

97   "its deepest humiliation": Weyr account, p. 74.

97   "hour of my life": Toland, p. 483.

99   "retreat from danger": S. Freud, *The Ego and the Id, SE*, vol. 19, p. 56.

101 "form of action": S. Freud, *Group Psychology, SE*, vol. 18, p. 117.

102 "and fantastic hopes": Bullock, p. 219.

104 "the unconscious mind": cited by Molnar, p. 233–4.

106 "I no longer": *Letters*, p. 442.

106 "sorry for you": cited by Gay, p. 170.

108 "stuff of work": Gay, p. 384.

110 "see no sign": cited by Toland, p. 488.

112 "a kind of longing": cited by Gay, p. 612.

113 "all-controlling factor": Paskauskas, ed., p. 763.

113 "die in freedom": *Letters*, p. 443.

116 "to the Gestapo": M. Freud, p. 216.

121 "Anna brought along": *Letters*, p. 445.

122 "the Gestapo to everyone": Gay, p. 628.

124 "he feels ill": S. Freud, *Ego and the Id, SE*, vol. 19, p. 49–50.

126 "have been abandoned": Hitler, p. 42.

London

For the story of Freud's life in London, the book again draws on Gay, Jones, and Molnar, and also on Max Schur's *Freud: Living and Dying*. For historical background, the section makes use of Peter F. Clarke's *Hope and Glory* and Piers Brendon's *The Dark Valley*, as well as contemporary accounts by Winston Churchill and A. J. P. Taylor. For events on the continent, Evans's *Third Reich in Power* is again the most prominent source.

137 "be a pandemonium": cited by Porter, p. 338.

138 "had secretly cherished": Taylor, p. 419.

138 "heroes of 'the kikes'": Graves and Hodge, p. 439.

140 "accomplish any work": *Letters*, p. 446.

140 "after English views": cited by Gay, p. 31.

140 "with my nature": cited by Davies et al., p. 9–10.

141 "the first weeks": *Letters*, p. 447.

141 "what fame means": ibid., p. 448.

144 "than a Jew": S. Freud, "The Resistances to Psycho-analysis," *SE*, vol. 19, p. 222.

145 "the completed essay secret": *Letters*, p. 422.

145 "be very offended": ibid., p. 440.

148 "there is nothing new": Van den Berg, p. 176.

149 "as he can": cited by Molnar, p. 240.

150 "heredity and upbringing": Jones, vol. 3, p. 234.

151 "his human weakness": S. Freud, *The Future of an Illusion, SE*, vol. 21 p. 24.

152 "shall take place": ibid., p. 30.

153 "have been abandoned": Hitler, p. 42.

154 "worthy of it": Nietzsche, *Gay Science*, p. 181.

158 "But *quien sabe*": Paskauskas, ed., p. 763.

162 "'come to something'": S. Freud, *Interpretation of Dreams, SE*, vol. 4, p. 216.

163 "that affects me": S. Freud, "The Moses of Michelangelo," *SE*, vol. 13, p. 211.

164 "on the stones": ibid., p. 229–230.

165 "has devoted himself": ibid., p. 233.

167 "the Hotel Sacher": Dalí, p. 23. For Dalí's meeting with Freud, see pp. 23–5.

168 "sentence on surrealism": ibid., p. 397.

169 "sharply from reality": S. Freud, "Creative Writers and Day-Dreaming," *SE*, vol. 9, p. 144.

169 "of his phantasies": ibid., p. 153.

172 "the medical curriculum": *The Question of Lay Analysis, SE,* vol. 20, p. 247.

173 "harder to reach": Schur, p. 508.

175 "number so-and-so": Brod, p. 204.

175 "what it all means": Paskauskas, ed., pp. 527–8.

175 "and lingual (tongue) mucous membranes": Schur, pp. 362–5.

176 "distress and pain": Jones, vol. 3, p. 95.

176 "in cruel mockery": Koestler, p. 498.

177 "combination of both": Schur, p. 364.

178 "of the fourth": *Letters,* p. 451.

179 "given his word": Toland, p. 502.

180 "we know nothing": Churchill, p. 283.

181 "pleasure in it": *Letters,* p. 452.

181 "it is *magic*": McGuire, ed., p. 117–8.

183 "cup and lip": cited by Molnar, p. 247.

187 "parasitic Jewish race": for an account of Kristallnacht, see Evans, pp. 590–592.

187 "Jewish filthy fellow": Gilbert, p. 55.

189 "out of Czechoslovakia": ibid., p. 216.

189 "involved than myself": S. Freud, "Anti-Semitism in England," *SE,* vol. 23, p. 301.

190 "duty to them": S. Freud, "Comment on Anti-Semitism," *SE,* vol. 23, p. 292.

190 "spirit of it": Twain, p. 358.

194 "gentleness, great strength": Woolf, pp. 168–9.

195 "for possible crumbs": Bell, ed., p. 202.

196 "with outstretched arm": Woolf, p. 191.

196 "in selected cases": Schur, p. 499. For more on Sauerwald, see Murray G. Hall, "The Fate of the Internationaler Psychoanalytischer Verlag," in Timms and Segal, eds.

198 "must risk it": *Letters,* p. 453–4.

199 "published it in defiance": Gay, p. 648.

199 "one of them": S. Freud, *Moses and Monotheism, SE,* vol. 23, p. 7.

200 "the real one": ibid., p. 15.

203 For the reviews of *Moses and Monotheism*, see Gay, pp. 645–8.

206 "prove the stronger": E. Freud, *Letters of Freud and Zweig*, p. 178.

206 "sort except aspirin": cited in Schur, p. 525.

208 "a fetid odor": ibid.

210 "is repeating it": S. Freud, "Remembering, Repeating and Working Through," *SE*, vol. 12, p. 150.

211 "to our intervention": ibid., p. 154.

213 "and the outside": Schur, p. 526 and 527.

216 "foresaw . . . that future": M. Freud, p. 16.

217 "inside an enigma": Churchill, p. 403.

221 "a few people": S. Freud, *Civilization and Its Discontents*, *SE*, vol. 21, pp. 79–80.

224 " 'rest is silence' ": Jones, vol. 3, p. 246.

225 " 'I thank you' ": Schur, p. 529.

227 "King Macbeth says": E. Freud and Meng, ed., *Psychoanalysis and Faith*, p. 35.

228 "carried forth everywhere": Nietzsche, *Human, All too Human*, p. 125.

230 Phillips's essay appears in *Darwin's Worms*, pp. 67–111.

232 "necessary psychological consequences": S. Freud, *Moses and Monotheism, SE*, vol. 23, pp. 112–13.

234 "their secret treasure": ibid., p. 115.

Selected Bibliography

Arendt, Hannah. *The Origins of Totalitarianism.* New York: Schocken Books, 1948.

Balzac, Honoré de. *The Wild Ass's Skin.* Translated by Herbert J. Hunt. New York: Penguin Books, 1977.

Behling, Katja. *Martha Freud: A Biography.* Translated by R. D. V. Glasgow. Cambridge, England, and Malden, MA: Polity Press, 2005.

Bell, Anne Olivier, ed. *The Diary of Virginia Woolf.* Vol. 5, 1936–1941. San Diego, New York, and London: Harcourt Brace & Company, 1984.

Berman, Paul. *Terror and Liberalism.* New York: W. W. Norton, 2003.

Bertin Célia. *Marie Bonaparte: A Life.* New Haven: Yale University Press, 1982.

Blom, Philipp. *To Have and to Hold: An Intimate History of Collectors and Collecting.* Woodstock and New York: Overlook Press, 2003.

Bonaparte, Marie. *Topsy: The Story of a Golden-Haired Chow.* New Brunswick, NJ: Transaction, 1994.

Bowie, Malcolm. *Lacan.* Cambridge, MA: Harvard University Press, 1991.

Brabant, Eva, Ernst Falzeder, and Patrizia Giampieri-Deutsch, eds. *The Correspondence of Sigmund Freud and Sándor Ferenczi,* Vol. 1, 1908–1914. Translated by Peter Hoffer. Cambridge, MA: Belknap Press of Harvard University Press, 1993.

Breger, Louis. *Sigmund Freud: Darkness in the Midst of Vision.* New York: John Wiley and Sons, 2000.

Brendon, Piers. *The Dark Valley: A Panorama of the 1930s.* New York: Alfred A. Knopf, 2000.

Brod, Max. *Franz Kaflka: A Biography.* New York: Schocken Books, 1947.

Brome, Vincent. *Ernest Jones: A Biography.* New York: W. W. Norton, 1983.

Brook-Shepherd, Gordon. *Anschluss: The Rape of Austria.* Westport, CT: Greenwood Press, 1976.

Bullock, Alan. *Hitler and Stalin: Parallel Lives.* New York: Random House, 1991.

Churchill, Winston S. *The Gathering Storm.* Vol. 1, *The Second World War.* Boston: Houghton Mifflin, 1948.

Clare, George. *Last Waltz in Vienna: The Rise and Destruction of a Family, 1842–1942.* New York: Holt, Rinehart and Winston, 1980.

Clark, Ronald W. *Freud, the Man and His Cause.* London: Jonathan Cape and Weidenfeld and Nichols, 1980.

Clarke, Peter F. *Hope and Glory: Britain 1900–1990.* London: Penguin Press, 1996.

Cocks, Geoffry. *Psychotherapy in the Third Reich: The Göring Institute*, 2nd ed. New Brunswick, NJ, and London: Transaction, 1997.

Dalí, Salvador. *The Secret Life of Salvador Dalí.* Translated by Haakon M. Chevalier. London: Vision Press, 1948.

Davies, Erica, J. Keith Davies, Michael Molnar, Susan O'Cleary, Ivan Ward. *20 Maresfield Gardens: A Guide to the Freud Museum.* London: Freud Museum, 1998.

DeLillo, Don. *White Noise.* New York: Viking, 1985.

H.D. [Doolittle, Hilda]. *Tribute to Freud.* New York: Pantheon, 1956.

Edmundson, Mark. *Towards Reading Freud: Self-Creation in Milton, Wordsworth, Emerson, and Sigmund Freud.* Princeton, NJ: Princeton University Press, 1990.

Engelman, Edmund. *Berggasse 19: Sigmund Freud's Home and Offices, Vienna 1938.* Chicago and London: University of Chicago Press, 1976.

Erdman, David V., and Harold Bloom, eds. *The Complete Poetry and Prose of William Blake.* New York: Random House, 1988.

Evans, Richard J. *The Third Reich in Power, 1933–1939.* New York: Penguin Press, 2005.

Fine, Reuben. *A History of Psychoanalysis.* New York: Columbia University Press, 1979.

Freud, Ernst L. *Letters of Sigmund Freud.* Translated by Tania and James Stern. New York: Basic Books, 1960.

Freud, Ernst L., ed. *The Letters of Sigmund Freud and Arnold Zweig.* Translated by Elaine and William D. Robson-Scott. New York: Harcourt, Brace & World, 1970.

Freud, Ernst L., Lucie Freud, and Ilse Grubrich-Simitis, eds. *Sigmund Freud: His Life in Pictures and Words.* Translated by Christine Trollope. New York: Harcourt Brace Jovanovich, 1978.

Freud Ernst L., and Heinrich Meng. *Psychoanalysis and Faith: The Letters of Sigmund Freud and Oskar Pfister,* translated by Eric Mosbacher. London: Hogarth Press, 1963.

Freud, Martin. *Sigmund Freud: Man and Father.* New York and London: Jason Aronson, 1983.

Friedrich, Otto. *Before the Deluge: A Portrait of Berlin in the 1920s.* New York: HarperCollins, 1972.

Gamwell, Lynn, and Richard Wells, eds. *Sigmund Freud and Art: His Personal Collection of Antiquities.* London: Freud Museum, 1989.

Gay, Peter. *Freud: A Life for Our Time.* New York: W. W. Norton, 1971.

Gedye, G. E. R. *Fallen Bastions: The Central European Tragedy.* London: Victor Gollancz, 1939.

Gilbert, Martin. *Kristallnacht: Prelude to Destruction.* London: Harper Press, 2006.

Goggin, James E., and Eileen Brockman Goggin. *Death of a "Jewish Science": Psychoanalysis in the Third Reich.* West Lafayette, IN: Purdue University Press, 2001.

Graves, Robert, and Alan Hodge. *The Long Week-End: A Social History of Great Britain, 1918–1939.* New York: Norton, 1940.

Hall, Murray G. "The Fate of the Internationaler Psychoanalytischer Verlag." In *Freud in Exile, Psychoanalysis and Its Vicissitudes.* Edited by Edward Timms and Naomi Segal. New Haven, CT: Yale University Press, 1988.

Hamann, Brigitte. *Hitler's Vienna: A Dictator's Apprenticeship.* Translated by Thomas Thornton. New York: Oxford University Press, 1999.

Hitler, Adolf. *Mein Kampf.* Translated by Ralph Manheim. Boston: Houghton Mifflin, 1943.

Huss, Pierre. *Heil and Farewell.* London: Jenkins, 1943.

Janik, Allan, and Stephen Toulmin. *Wittgenstein's Vienna.* New York: Simon and Schuster, 1973.

Jones, Ernest. *The Life and Work of Sigmund Freud.* 3 vols. New York: Basic Books, 1957.

Jung, Carl G. *Memories, Dreams, Reflections.* New York: Pantheon, 1963.

Keegan, John. *The First World War.* New York: Random House, 1998.

Kershaw, Ian. *Hitler: 1936–1945 Nemesis.* New York: W. W. Norton, 2000.

————. *Making Friends with Hitler: Lord Londonderry, the Nazis and the Road to World War II.* New York: Penguin Press, 2004.

Koestler, Arthur. *The Invisible Writing: The Second Volume of an Autobiography: 1932–1940.* London: Hutchinson & Company, 1954.

Kubizek, August. *The Young Hitler I Knew.* Translated by E. V. Anderson. Westport, CT: Greenwood Press, 1954.

Mann, Thomas. *Freud, Goethe, Wagner.* New York: Alfred A. Knopf, 1937.

Marx, Karl, and Friedrich Engels. *The Communist Manifesto.* New York: Penguin, 1967.

Masson, Jeffrey, M., ed. and trans. *The Complete Letters of Sigmund Freud to Wilhelm Fliess, 1887–1904.* Cambridge, MA: Belknap Press of Harvard University Press, 1985.

McGuire, William, ed. *The Freud / Jung Letters: The Correspondence Between Sigmund Freud and C. G. Jung.* Translated by Ralph Manheim and R. F. C. Hull. Princeton, NJ: Princeton University Press, 1974.

McGuire, William, and R. F. C. Hull, eds. *C.G. Jung Speaking.* Princeton, NJ: Princeton University Press, 1977.

Miller, Jonathan, ed. *Freud: The Man, His World, His Influence.* Boston and Toronto: Little, Brown & Company, 1972.

Molnar, Michael, ed. and trans. *The Diary of Sigmund Freud, 1929–1939: A Record of the Final Decade.* New York: Charles Scribner's Sons, 1992.

Nietzsche, Freidrich. *The Gay Science.* Translated by Walter Kaufmann. New York: Vintage Books, 1974.

—————. *Human, All Too Human: A Book for Free Spirits*. Translated by Marion Faber with Stephen Lehmann. Lincoln: University of Nebraska Press, 1986.

Paskauskas, R. Andrew, ed. *The Complete Correspondence of Sigmund Freud and Ernest Jones, 1908–1939*. Cambridge, MA: Harvard University Press, 1993.

Payne, Robert. *The Life and Death of Adolf Hitler*. New York and Washington, DC: Praeger Publishers, 1973.

Pfeiffer, Ernst, ed. *Sigmund Freud and Lou Andreas-Salomé: Letters*. Translated by William D. Robson-Scott and Elaine Robson-Scott. New York: W. W. Norton, 1985.

Phillips, Adam. *Darwin's Worms*. London: Faber and Faber, 1999.

—————. *Equals*. New York: Basic Books, 2002.

—————. *Terrors and Experts*. London: Faber and Faber, 1995.

Porter, Roy. *London: A Social History*. Cambridge, MA: Harvard University Press, 1994.

Rickels, Laurence A. *Nazi Psychoanalysis Vol. 1, Only Psychoanalysis Won the War*. Minneapolis and London: University of Minnesota Press, 2002.

Rieff, Philip. *Freud: The Mind of the Moralist*. Chicago: University of Chicago Press, 1959.

Roazen, Paul. *Edoardo Weiss: The House that Freud Built*. New Brunswick, NJ, and London: Transaction, 2005.

—————. *Freud and His Followers*. New York: Alfred A. Knopf, 1975.

Romm, Sharon. *The Unwelcome Intruder: Freud's Struggle with Cancer*. New York: Praeger, 1983.

Rosenbaum, Ron. *Explaining Hitler: The Search for the Origins of Evil*. New York: Random House, 1998.

Rosenzweig, Saul. *The Historic Expedition to America: Freud, Jung and Hall the King-Maker*. St. Louis: Rana House, 1994.

Said, Edward W. *Freud and the Non-European*. London and New York: Verso, 2003.

Schmidt, Elfrede. *1938 . . . and the Consequences*. Translated by Peter L. Lyth. Riverside, CA: Ariadne Press, 1992.

Schorske, Carl E. *Fin-De-Siècle Vienna: Politics and Culture.* New York: Random House, 1981.

Schur, Max. *Freud: Living and Dying.* New York: International Universities Press, 1972.

Schuschnigg, Kurt von. *Austrian Requiem.* Translated by Franz von Hildebrand. New York: G. P. Putnam Sons, 1946.

Shirer, William L. *Berlin Diary: The Journal of a Foreign Correspondent, 1934–1941.* New York: Alfred A. Knopf, 1941.

Smith, Dennis Mack. *Mussolini: A Biography.* New York: Alfred A. Knopf, 1982.

Sontag, Susan. *Under the Sign of Saturn.* New York: Farrar, Straus, Giroux, 1980.

Steiner, George. *The Portage to San Cristobal of A.H.* New York: Simon and Schuster, 1981.

Strachey, James, et al., eds. *The Standard Edition of the Complete Psychological Works of Sigmund Freud,* 24 vols. London: Hogarth Press, 1953–1974.

Taylor, A. J. P. *English History, 1914–1945.* Oxford: Clarendon Press, 1965.

Toland, John. *Adolf Hitler.* 2 vols. Garden City, NY: Doubleday, 1976.

Trevor-Roper, Hugh. *The Last Days of Hitler.* Chicago: University of Chicago Press, 1971.

Twain, Mark. *Collected Tales, Sketches, Speeches and Essays, 1891–1910.* New York: Library of America, 1992.

Unwerth, Matthew von. *Freud's Requiem: Mourning, Memory, and the Invisible History of a Summer Walk.* New York: Riverhead Books, 2005.

Van den Berg, Jan Hendrich. *The Changing Nature of Man: Introduction to a Historical Psychology.* Translated by H. F. Croes. New York, Delta, 1961.

Weyr, Thomas. *The Setting of the Pearl: Vienna Under Hitler.* Oxford: Oxford University Press, 2005.

Woolf, Leonard. *Downhill All the Way: An Autobiography of the Years 1919–1939.* London: Hogarth Press, 1967.

Wright, William E., ed. *Austria, 1938–1988: Anschluss and Fifty Years.* Riverside, CA: Ariadne Press, 1995.

Yerushalmi, Yosef Hayim. *Freud's Moses: Judaism Terminable and Interminable.* New Haven, CT, and London: Yale University Press, 1991.

Young-Bruehl, Elisabeth. *Anna Freud: A Biography.* New York: Summit, 1988.

Zaretsky, Eli. *Secrets of the Soul: A Social and Cultural History of Psychoanalysis.* New York: Random House, 2004.

Zweig, Stefan. *The World of Yesterday.* Lincoln: University of Nebraska Press, 1943.

Index

A Note on the Author

Mark Edmundson teaches at the University of Virginia, where he holds the rank of University Professor. A prizewinning scholar, he has published a number of works of literary and cultural criticism, including *Literature Against Philosophy, Plato to Derrida, Teacher: The One Who Made the Difference,* and *Why Read?* He has also written for such publications as *Raritan,* the *New Republic,* the *New York Times Magazine,* the *Nation,* and *Harper's,* where he is a contributing editor.

A Note on the Type

The text of this book is set Adobe Garamond. It is one of several versions of Garamond based on the designs of Claude Garamond. It is thought that Garamond based his font on Bembo, cut in 1495 by Francesco Griffo in collaboration with the Italian printer Aldus Manutius. Garamond types were first used in books printed in Paris around 1532. Many of the present-day versions of this type are based on the *Typi Academiae* of Jean Jannon cut in Sedan in 1615.

Claude Garamond was born in Paris in 1480. He learned how to cut type from his father and by the age of fifteen he was able to fashion steel punches the size of a pica with great precision. At the age of sixty he was commissioned by King Francis I to design a Greek alphabet, for this he was given the honorable title of royal type founder. He died in 1561.